THE
LASCAUX PRIZE
2017

THE
LASCAUX PRIZE
2017

edited by
Camille Griep
Stephen Parrish
Wendy Russ

ISBN 10: 0-9851666-6-5
ISBN 13: 978-0-9851666-6-3

Cover design by Wendy Russ.
Cover art by Vasily Polenov: "Overgrown Pond," oil on canvas, 1879.

Lascaux Books
www.lascauxbooks.com

Contents

continued next page

Poetry Finalists

Short Story Winner

Short Story Finalists

Editor's Choice Awards

Introduction

Welcome to the fourth edition of *The Lascaux Prize Anthology*. Nine flash pieces lead off this volume, followed by fifteen poems and eight full-length stories, all winners or finalists in our annual literary contests. We close with three works of creative nonfiction selected from our online journal.

Each piece has something to share, whether a powerful message ("Heathen at Thanksgiving" and "Heaven"), a poignant observation ("Cheerleaders Practicing in Eveleth MN," "If I Have a Daughter," and "Object of Art"), a hauntingly vivid tale ("The Emigrants"), brilliant satire ("Cry on Command"), heart-in-the-throat suspense ("Safety"), or a heart wrenching story ("Rocket Night," "Jackie," and "The Other Baby"). We trust if you sample the contents you'll find enough compelling literature to keep you up late reading.

Fifteen of the thirty-five pieces in this volume—nearly half—appeared elsewhere before finding their way to our contests and into our journal. We remain committed to the idea that a piece of writing needn't be set aside merely because someone else discovered it first.

An anthology of this kind is necessarily an eclectic gathering of unrelated pieces. There is no unifying theme. Yet like the children of a large family, the pieces function well together, despite having their individual quirks and temperaments. They compliment one another. Maybe we, the editors, have assembled something coherent after all, a product of our mutual taste in literature as well as a small reflection of the time in which we live. Hopefully years from now writers will examine gatherings such as ours and enjoy glimpses of their forebears.

Our purpose in this anthology has been the same as in our previous efforts, to discover quality writing, to acknowledge it, to bring it to light.

Camille Griep
Stephen Parrish
Wendy Russ

Rocket Night
by Alexander Weinstein

It was Rocket Night at our daughter's elementary school, the night when parents, students, and administrators gather to place the least-liked child in a rocket and shoot him into the stars. Last year we placed Laura Jackson into the capsule, a short, squat girl known for the limp dresses that hung crookedly on her body. The previous year we'd sent off a boy from India whose name none of us could remember.

Rocket Night falls in late October when the earth is covered by leaves. Our children have begun to lay out their Halloween costumes and their sweaters are heavy with the scent of autumn. It's late enough into the school year for us to get a sense of the best children to send off. Alliances are made early at Rose Hill. Our children gather in the mornings to share secrets on the playground, while the other children—those with stars and galaxies in their futures—can be seen at the edges of the field, playing with sticks alone or staring into mud puddles at drowned worms.

In the school gymnasium, we mingle in the warm glow of lacquered floors, surrounded by wooden bleachers and parallel bars, talking about soccer games and the difficulty of errands with our children's busy schedules. Our kids run the perimeter, some playing tag, others collecting in clusters of boys around the fifth-graders with portable game consoles. Susan Beech brought her home-baked cupcakes, the Stowes brought Hawaiian Punch, and we brought plastic cups and placed them among the baked goods and apple slices.

The boy to be sent off stood near his parents, holding his mother's skirt. One could immediately see the reason he'd been chosen. The mildewed scent of thrift stores clung to his corduroys, and his collar sat askew, revealing the small white undershirt beneath. The boy, our daughter told us, brought stubby pencils to school whose chewed-up ends got stuck in sharpeners. He had the habit of picking his nose and wiping it on his pants. His lunches were nothing more than stale crackers and a warm box of chocolate milk. There was a smear of frosting on his mouth, and upon seeing this we knew our children had chosen well. He was the sort of child who makes one proud of one's own children, and we looked to our daughter, who was holding court with a devil's square, tightening then spreading her small fingers within the folded paper while counting out the letters O-R-A-N-G-E.

At eight o'clock the principal took the stage beneath the basketball hoop and welcomed us to another year at Rose Hill. He thanked Susan for her cupcakes, and all of us for our contributions to the evening's festivities. Then he turned to the family and said, "We hope your son's journey into space will be a joyful one." We all applauded. His parents applauded less than others, looking a bit pale, but parents of the chosen often seem pale. They are the sort of people who come to soccer games and sit alone in the stands, a gloomy sadness hanging over them which none of us wish to share.

His speech delivered, the principal invited us to join him on the playground where the capsule sat, its silver sides illuminated by the glow of the launch tower. It's a truth that the child to be sent into space grows reticent upon seeing the casket-like rocket. We saw the boy cling to his mother, unwilling to leave her side, and so we let our children loose. I watched my daughter pry the boy's fingers from his mother's leg as two larger fifth-graders seized his waist and dragged him away. The nurse helped to subdue the parents. She took the mother aside and whispered to her, while the gym coach placed a meaty hand on the father's shoulder and assured him the capsule was stocked with enough water and food tablets to last the boy long into the future. To be honest, it's a mystery how long such supplies last—we're all aware funding was cut to our district earlier this year—but still we assured them there was nothing to fear. The boy, if hungry for company, had a small microphone which would allow him to speak to himself about his journey and the mysteries of space.

The boy was strapped into the capsule, his hands secured, and he looked out at us. He spoke then, for the first and only time that night. He asked if he might have one of his pencils; it was in his pencil box, he said, the one with a brown bear eraser. The principal assured him he wouldn't need it in outer space, and the custodian noted the request was moot; the boy's desk had been emptied earlier that day. So they closed the cover. All we could see was the smudge of the boy's face pressed against the porthole.

When the rocket blasted off, it made us all take an involuntary step backwards, the light of the flames illuminating the wonder upon our children's faces. The capsule rose from the playground, leaving behind our swing sets and jungle gym, rising higher, until it was a sparkling marble in the night sky, and then, finally, gone. We sighed with awe, some applauded, and then we made our rounds, wishing one another goodnight, arranging play dates, and returning to our cars.

And the boy faded from our thoughts, replaced by the lateness of the evening and the pressure of delayed bedtime schedules. I myself had all but forgotten about the child by the time I laid our sleeping daughter on her bed. And yet, when I took out the recycling, I paused beneath the streetlamps of our cul-de-sac and thought of all the children high above. I imagined them drifting alone up there, speaking into their microphones, reporting to themselves about the depths of the unknown.

"Rocket Night" originally appeared in *Southern Indiana Review*.

Warning
by Alexandra Comeaux

I was expecting death to happen better, faster, from behind—like when someone else's husband pats your ass at the cocktail party, or when you crack a new wine glass on the floor and your father beats you half-deaf, saying *I told you not to, I told you not, I told you—*

—If you tilt a black eye toward everything being ripped out of you so fast, it's almost as if your mother is back at the barbecue, crying into Easter grass and asking for her purse. She wants to know what day it is. She wants another drink. She wants her kindergartner to drive her home—

But forget this. There is nothing at the center. Look how well I am fixed now: less than one-third of my day spent considering how to rid myself of the other two. I cartwheel to work, braid small children's hair on the lawn. I'm looking street performers in the eyes again, shaking sweaty hands at the pharmaceutical luncheon, wishing good fortune on your baby, the future engineer, saying *congratulations* and *my god, no, I can't believe how fast you lost the weight—*

"Warning" originally appeared in *Quarter After Eight*.

Family Dinner

by Valerie Cumming

I.

Food is important. It always has to mean something: ham on Easter, roast beef on Christmas. Served on my grandmother's good Lenox china, a wedding gift: real gold edging, with gold-plated utensils to match. My mother had wedding china once, but she broke it all against the kitchen floor one night when my father came home late. We were supposed to be in bed, Lucy and me, but who could sleep through that racket, him calling her a crazy bitch and her yelling *You want to see crazy? I can show you crazy.* And all the while, dishes going like the Fourth of July around his feet.

II.

It's important, no matter what, to clean your plate, even if the ham is pink like the pigs it came from, pink like little squealy piglets with springy, curly tails. Eat, they growl at you. Eat, or you can't get up from the table. Eat, or no dessert. But they themselves barely touch what's in front of them, either because they're dieting (the women) or they've had too much to drink (the men). They take their good china plates back to the kitchen and scrape them into the garbage disposal when they think no one's looking, except that I'm always looking.

III.

If you take an extra helping and you happen to be a girl, everyone's eyes are on you. They follow you back to the kitchen, push you up against the counter in what they pretend is a hug, all the while pinching at the extra flesh on your belly and hips. A girl your age, they say—teasing, smiling—a girl your age ought to watch her figure. Pretty little girl like you.

IV.

Lucy does it when she thinks no one's looking, but I am. I see the way she goes to the kitchen to scrape her plate into the trash, then pretends to be full. There was a girl like that at my school once: at lunchtime, instead of going to the cafeteria with the rest of us, she had to go to the nurse's office, where the aide fed her spoonfuls of applesauce and banana pudding and watched to make sure she didn't try to throw it all back up again. After a few months, this girl started to look less like a skeleton and was allowed to come back to the cafeteria a couple of times a week, and everyone wanted to sit with her. Just like that, she was the most popular girl in our grade.

Lucy doesn't look like a skeleton, but she's small for almost-eleven and her hands shake when she clears the table and her long hair looks like straw, not shiny anymore. There's less of her than there used to be, like she's slipping away a little bit at a time. Suddenly I start thinking about what it would be like if Lucy were that popular too, the most popular girl in school, and that makes me feel like hitting her. Instead, I threaten to tell. You're just trying to get attention, I whisper-yell, because being scared is making me mean.

Go ahead and tell, Lucy says, not looking up from the dishes, but I can see by the way she holds her thin bird shoulders that she's afraid.

But my mother is dancing: wine glass in one hand, the other wrapped around the wide shoulders of one of the uncles. They're dancing in my grandmother's living room, which is usually off-limits; they're leaving foot marks in the perfectly vacuumed white carpet. They're playing some old record of my grandfather's, the kind that sounds like elevator music, and my mother is crying and laughing at once while what's left of dinner congeals on the table.

Mom, I say. Come here a second. Lucy needs you.

But she's busy dancing, and pretends not to hear.

We Can Go Faster

by Kathryn Bucolo Hill

We go 95 on the road out of Ephrata because Alicia's dad left and her mom didn't hide the keys. The Amber Alerts have our plate number now. We didn't leave anybody notes. Alicia drives her dad's old blue truck, fast like he's under the wheels, like he's crunch-smeared into the highway, like tomato soup, a dead dog. She laughs because we're stealing ourselves. Our moms are probably crying.

Alicia says My mom's an idiot. Doesn't even know he wouldn't steal me.

The moon is out, a bright spoon. The engine yells hot, ostinato. I want to say Your dad would steal you. But I don't. Mine didn't steal me. We pass the exit sign for Brownstown. We pass Oregon Dairy.

Alicia says We can go faster.

I say How fast.

She says Faster.

I say Okay because she wrote a poem for school about red wrists in a tub. I can hear the metal legs of the engine, see the speedometer click 100. I think the number 100 is a needle and buttons, a needle and buttons to stitch her skin up when I find her grisly wristed, red in a tub somewhere in D.C. or New Jersey or wherever and I have to call her mom to tell her that she's dead, forget that the area code will give us away.

We go 100. We go 105. I watch the moon above the empty corn fields, watch it, remember my dad sipping gin in the summer, ice like clinking moons, remember him finding Cassiopeia in the clouds, Cassandra Martin despite her gold ring and his. Remember he left everything but took our kitchen table when he left with her for Oregon. Remember how the kitchen rug is fading in the sun.

I say What did your dad take.

She says Everything but us.

I see my dad crawling out of the median. Our tires turn him to fireworks.

I say We can go faster.

Alicia says Okay.

I click a fingernail under my skin, by my collarbone, slide it out red like a button.

Alicia says Make a necklace. She rolls up her sleeves, says See, I have bracelets.

I laugh. I don't think about anything. I dig my skin like engine pistons. I imagine us naked in a tub. Our phones are buzzing. It's not our dads. We chuck them in the back seat. We have duct tape to change the plate number. We have money in the pockets of our jeans. I wonder if Alicia would call my mom to tell her if I died. Maybe our moms are drunk, together. Maybe they'll be just fine. The moon is jaundiced. The moon is sick. We go 115 on the interstate.

"We Can Go Faster" originally appeared in *Fiction Southeast*.

The Other Baby
by Jackleen Holton

The Other Baby was born the same day as you. The temperature in the Central Valley had dropped to a record low. I scraped the frost off the windshield before I drove myself to the hospital. Your father was passed out in bed and I couldn't wake him. When I crossed the train tracks, I felt you hurtling toward me. I sped the rest of the way. They rushed me to the delivery room, and there you were, as if you'd been waiting the whole time. The doctor placed you in my arms, told me I was made for having children. In the morning, your grandma brought your father in. He held out the bundle of red roses she bought for me. Later that day, I heard the story from the nurses. It was a girl too, the other baby, wrapped in an old blanket, found frozen in a garbage dumpster. We took you home to the crib we'd set up in the living room. I held you and fed you as I watched the news. Annabelle was her name. She'd been eight pounds, same as you. I still remember her tiny coffin, the small group of mourners, nurses and social workers, huddled over it, their gloved hands held out as if it were a fire that could warm them. In the wind, the elm tree scraped the roof of our house. Your father snored in the bedroom. I wept and a tear fell onto your smooth red face. They never found Annabelle's mother. Your dad wrecked his yellow Corvette, got arrested and put in jail for three months. You woke me every night screaming. A few weeks after your third birthday, he passed out again and didn't wake up. After we moved to Arizona, you announced that you hated your name, refused to answer to it anymore. When you were fourteen, I had to rush you to the hospital to have your stomach pumped. Then at seventeen, you kicked me in the face. The police came, and you screamed you wished you were dead as they cuffed you and wrestled you away. I take pills to help me sleep, but every night, I run through alleys, fling open trash bins. I rummage through dirty blankets, uncover tiny blue faces, my hands and feet icy and bleeding. But I can't remember where I lost you.

"The Other Baby" originally appeared in *Permafrost.*

When Trapped in a Car Under Water
by Landon Houle

All these poems about mercy, these scenes of fathers and animals suffering on the road, remind me of my own dad and those nights he drove us grille-first down the boat ramp.

We couldn't afford a boat, of course. Once, though, at Sandy Creek Marina, we played make-believe. He ran his chapped hand down a Stingray with a ruby-slipper stripe and played the possibility. I played like I believed him. I believed it was the salesman we were tricking.

To launch a boat, you drive in reverse. You ease down the ramp until the water is just above the trailer hubs. But without a trailer and without a boat, only a family of three in a rusted Chevy edges closer and closer still until the dirty lake—black at night—laps against the tires, and I'd like to believe he was a few in. I'd like to explain by saying he was drunker than a skunk and stoned out of his mind. If this were true, I'd tell you something besides the way the headlights shone on the water and how, if you could trick yourself, you might think something beautiful glittered there just beneath the surface.

But if I'm honest, I'll say he was never as sober as when the cab began taking in water, when the water came up to our ankles. He was never more clear-headed than those nights when my mother pressed my face to her chest, and when I remember, I remember her screams, but when I dream, I dream the truth. I was the one screaming. My mother was quiet. My mother never said a word, and through the pillow, through the soft flannel of her nightgown, I hear nothing but the beat and this as steady as ever.

In the poems about mercy, a father does what's best. He brains the porcupine. He drags the hazard of a doe, unborn fawn be damned, off the road and pushes her into the river, and I don't know that the water is black anymore than I know this man is a father, but there are truths you only imagine, realities you dream to understand.

The choice is never easy, and I wonder if it was more difficult for my father to drive into the water or out of it. I wonder which direction felt more like a kindness to a man whose face shone as dark as a night lake.

I'd like to read more poems about fathers who let porcupines live, fathers who open their coats to bloody fawns. There, too, in the beat or—better yet—the caesura should be a silent mother, a manual about what to do when trapped in a car under water. In my dreams, we bust glass with our fingertips. We reach out and touch something beautiful. All we have to do is wait. All we have to do is stay calm.

"When Trapped in a Car Under Water" originally appeared in *The Baltimore Review.*

The Glove
by Ronald Jackson

I came down the stairs, irked that I couldn't fasten the clasp at the back of my blouse. My husband sat in front of his computer in our breakfast nook, eating breakfast and absorbed in his baseball chat. They called for rain on the TV yesterday, and outside our bay window, the back yard darkened.

A half-eaten piece of toast clung to the egg yolk on his plate, and a raggedy baseball glove rested at his elbow. On his walk home from the El last night, he'd found it in an empty lot, nestled in some dead weeds.

Now he picked up the glove and reversed its shape. A wet stain made the pocket glisten. A can of neats foot oil, the kind people use to soften leather, stood next to the glove, and he'd draped a yellow-stained rag over the can. *Derek Jeter* was inscribed along the thumb. My husband and Chase hated the Yankees.

I asked him to help me with my blouse, and he got up and did it without a word. I asked if maybe we shouldn't put the glove back someplace prominent, with a sign attached. He sat down and resumed working the oil in.

My husband used to notice when I was having trouble getting dressed. He'd spring up quick and say something like, "Here, let me do that." Then he'd add, "Butterfingers!" in a smiley voice. I always got a little squeeze or a kiss on the back of the neck, while I stood still like a schoolgirl.

I sat down in the booth across from my husband, looked out at our tiny yard where Chase used to play. Last fall, before he'd been diagnosed, our son stood in the grass, near where my husband knelt alongside the narrow strip of garden we had along the back fence. He threw the ball in the air, flicked his glove awkwardly each time the ball came down, ran on about how the Phillies lost the night before. His father tossed the baseball back to Chase whenever it rolled near him.

My husband kept massaging the oil in as if I wasn't there. I had to do something, so I went to the garage and fished out my son's glove and a scuffed-up baseball from our sports bin. I tried the glove on, and it fit. I was going to miss my group, but I didn't care.

Back at the nook, my husband continued to work the oil in, ignoring me. I wasn't having it. I leaned over him from behind and lifted the glove from his hands. When he saw two gloves, he gave me a startled look. I led him down the back stoop, and a damp breeze blew across the yard. I handed him his glove and the ball, and he tossed it in the air and caught it with a smooth motion. It began to mist, and I put on Chase's glove. We played catch without a word as the mist became a light drizzle. The ball got soaked and I muffed the last of his soft tosses.

I took off my glove, slipped his off too, dropped the gloves and ball on the wet ground. A piece of cowhide cover stuck out from the ball like an ear. I pulled him tight against me, and he laid his forehead on my shoulder. His arms hung lifelessly. Then my husband draped his arms over my shoulders, pressed his cheek to mine, and whispered, "Butterfingers." The rain came harder, and we stood that way for what seemed like the whole morning.

Fifteen Silver Shillings
by Ríona Judge McCormack

1842, Aughnacloy

Fifteen silver shillings, that is the price. The mill overseer counts them into McCann's hand, bright from the mint. New coins for the dead.

"You're lucky," says the overseer. "They pay only twelve up at Dunbar's."

The dead child's age will go down in the book as ten; this is a lie.

In the scutching room, the men at the flax rollers are coughing and feeding, feeding and coughing. Wooden blades whick up and down. McCann sits at his berth and gathers the retted stems from his load and the other men do not raise their eyes to his. Beneath the blades and the pump of the shaft, there is the groaning of the great wheel turning. The coins weigh heavy in his pocket.

The dead child has been washed of dust from the flax-mill and laid out on the table. A cloth covers the worst of the wheel's damage. McCann brings a stool to the child's side.

When she comes in from the bleaching fields, McCann's wife holds out a reddened palm.

"John," she says, when he does not move. "Where is it?"

"I threw it away."

"Away where?"

"In the river."

She strikes him then, hard across the mouth. McCann raises his forearms over his face. His lip is cut; he tongues blood from it. When he lowers his arms, she is gone.

In the corner, the living child stirs the fire and is silent.

He finds her wet to her skirts in the river, searching. In turned-up sleeves he wades in alongside her. The water is winter-cold.

Together, they retrieve nine of the shillings. In the dark, on his knees, he wrings out her heavy skirts. He can feel her shiver against him.

She holds his elbow back across the Mulcahy fields, to where the fire from their own cabin shows like a light at sea.

"We will name the next one John," she says. Upstream, unseen, the millwheel grinds on.

"Fifteen Silver Shillings" was originally published by the Highlands and Islands Short Story Association.

The Gold
by Darren Morris

The sad little troopers in the minivan had finished last in the annual agricultural theater competition. One of the boys in Pack 302 still wore his stalk of corn costume. He had been corn. It was a part with no lines, none whatsoever.

Another boy's face was painted red. He had been a tomato.

"God I could use a fucking cigarette," the tomato said.

"Tommy," the den mother said, "I don't think you should be making jokes in front of the other boys."

"—fuck do you care? We blew it."

"You all did very well."

"We could have earned a gold, Mom. A fucking gold. Do you know what that means?"

"Tommy dear, please, the other boys."

The corn was crying, blubbering. He couldn't even cry correctly.

"It was the corn," the tomato said.

"Now, Tommy."

The tomato turned toward the corn.

"All you had to do was stand there."

The corn made a little spot of urine in his blue pants and the green leaf husk shook with wretchedness.

"You were fucking wallpaper, man. Now we're gonna have to make knot boards or some shit. You know how much I hate knot boards?"

"Let 'im alone," said the boy who'd been the farmer. He wore overalls and a corncob pipe poked out from his breast pocket. This was the boy who later hanged himself from the top bunk in his dormitory room. And when the corn would learn of it, just before he graduated himself, he would try not to remember how he'd lost the gold, or the spot blossoming on his pants, or the red-faced tomato, or the slip knot tied neatly around the farmer's wordless throat.

Cheerleaders Practicing
in Eveleth MN
by David Salner

The sky is a stone-cold blue, a late-summer blue.

In the North Country, there are blues so perfect
you want to tear your heart out to be alive
and sober. And the cheerleaders of Eveleth High
are stamping their feet in the cinders, wearing
flip-flops, pumps, tennis shoes, sandals.

They maintain a businesslike, a gum-chewing calm
as they rehearse the difficult moves, like the toss,
which must be perfect, and the even more difficult catch—
with a strength not in their arms, which are slender,
and not in their conditioning, which is nonexistent. I don't

blame them. Last night was a good one to spend
on the lakes with their friends and a case of beer.
Those lakes, some glacial, some quarried out.
Those lakes in the North Country, that perfect sky—
it's enough to make you get sober or try

or cry. But when Shelly Jongewaard flies in the air,
she knows that whatever else in the rest of her life
could go wrong, and probably will, the arms
of those girls from Eveleth High will always
be there, under the stone cold blue of the sky,

locked in a basket to catch her.

"Cheerleaders Practicing in Eveleth MN" originally appeared in
Southern Humanities Review.

A Precise Small Thing
by Lauren Camp

I didn't know I would run out of time to memorize
your voice. After three days trying, I just now remember
the name of a trombonist I heard three years ago,
and you have been missing 3,322 days.

Dad laughed when I asked for the recording of you
saying *no one is home right now* with your wine-sopped,
grass-pure voice. I can't remember it at all, that voice.

Not the strange wide way you had of stretching Ws
or the laugh that started from a precise small thing
and rolled on and on, expanding into time
we didn't realize was ending.

Or the way you called to us, your voice becoming a near
shriek in the almost dark, our names as large as puppets
expected to move back into that box of home again.

Or how you said *Dad.* Just that one word.
How you cried at the supper table some nights,
your voice turning into salt and red breath.

How you moaned gently. How your voice in my hands
expired into something I could no longer hear,
something smaller than atoms.

"A Precise Small Thing" originally appeared in *This Business of Wisdom* (West End Press).

Her Husband Considers the Words of Picasso

by Jeremy Cantor

Disciples be damned. It's not interesting. It's only the masters that matter. —Pablo Picasso, quoted in *De Renoir à Picasso,* Michel George-Michel, 1954

The candle light's too dim for me to read
your papers scattered on the kitchen table
but even in full daylight I would not
be able to understand the things that you
know more about than anyone else alive.
All of it will die the day you die.
You have no disciples.

But now that you are talking of your work
I won't interrupt you just to tell you
that without you
my life would be a language without metaphor

and I won't interrupt you just to say
that I can't stop myself from thinking about
the fire that still burns behind your eyes,
about your hands, your hair, your lips, your breasts
and about this candle going out.

I Read in the New York Times
by Marie Chambers

Music will always be your ornament
said the father to his daughter
as he hurled the stone that killed her

saffron robed sparrow of the clipped wing
soaring out loud not allowed
in these birdcage skies

clouds reach down to the land where she sang
wash her bloody shadow from the sand
drown the cries of her sisters

the past devours the present again
murderers abandon her corpse
antiquated music continues

there is no balm in her silence
no reasoning with tradition
you old bastard

Heathens at Thanksgiving
by Joseph Dante

after Kitty Tsui

I didn't tell you who was coming to dinner.
too bad. you'd meet him anyway:

this is my *partner*, shake his hand
with freckles like constellations of cinnamon
although you probably think of lepers and curses
and stains and animal heads hanging on doors.

my dear sister is the first and only to take
his hand and smile. her tight hug of tattoos
and bangled arms are a welcome home
greeting us like a breeze in our chimes.

this is my partner, i say,
his music fills small rooms, enough
for claps to be the chorus, enough for me—

if i knew he was coming, mamma says, if i *knew*.

but there are always leftovers anyway. nonna slices
and bastes the turkey, auntie smashes potatoes for
my cousin's gravy volcano, mamma bakes apple pie.
everything is homemade except the cranberry sauce,
which always appears without being acknowledged—

please don't let a tart side dish be a metaphor
for our relationship at every gathering. please,
don't let this become my prayer before the meal.

you: the sweating patriarch at the head of this table,
poking at a plate. where is your insatiable hunger?
why are you not shoving that big piece of meat in
your mouth without asking where it came from?

this is my partner,
he teaches and we'll have a house soon.
we'll have Surinam cherry and lychee trees.
you should come see the butterflies sometime.

let us keep some new rituals
with the feelings of the old,
like how we pretended to savor the host,
like how you taught me to spell tabernacle,
like how you crafted wings for me
to be a saint on stage.

you must admit how pagan everything is already:
votive candles, mosaics, hymnals, pearly amulets,
drinking wine and transfiguring bread as body
for renewal. magic never seemed so fertile.

so strange to see
stigmata and emaciated torso above
your crown at every sumptuous feast.
the meek shall inherit absolutely nothing.

touching my partner's hand,
i turn to auntie for astrology advice:
we are gemini and libra, we
read the air like a book between us, we
are cartographers of the same cloudscapes, we
disturb celestial alignment with our affinities.

auntie inhales, waits
for any small interruption.
i refuse silence to be the sole heirloom
i pass down to my children, and i refuse
to be buried with it.

this is my partner,
we would not have a big wedding
but how lopsided the affair would look:
his side full of wide-eyed cousins
from across the States, two beaming mothers,
three stepbrothers who'd shake hands,
and a dad who'd cry while giving a speech.
and my side: only a sister
giving a playful wink and a mamma
giving a slight nod.

let us have flowers and a rainbow cathedral
but banish any idea of sin or repentance.
without genuflecting, we can exalt
a unity we needn't explain.

bless me father, for i grew
into myself too early. i was
not a tiny effigy of you to pray on
like a rosary between your knuckles.

a single prayer of mine could be
answered with just a sound.
i look at your glistening forehead,
those tufts of wheat hair, and i wonder
if you intend for your gurgled yell
to be an exorcism or an exiling.

i think of the dream where a raven
emerges from your throat, speaking
in a human voice that isn't your own.
i take off my engagement ring
and let it become a shiny morsel
for you to finally swallow.

If I Have a Daughter
by April Ford

I.

If I have a daughter,
I will tell her
that by age sweet sixteen
she will most definitely
be fondled by a man.
Not a stranger—
strangers are only dangerous
if you follow them,
and my daughter won't be a follower
—but his touch will feel strange,
even if in her burgeoning fantasy life
it was meant to be.
My daughter will be stunning;
men will start watching her before she's fourteen.
Her shoulders will change hands
from inelegant fathering types with Donald Trump hair
to intentional types who convert girls to women for sport.
I will be honest when my daughter asks about men.
When she asks:

Mother, how did I come to be?
Did you make me out of rose petals and moonbeams?
I will assure her he's not like them, her father,
at least not as long as I've known him,
and does it really matter what he was like before then?
We can excuse those behaviors of men
before we know them as our fathers, brothers, or lovers.
Can't we?

II.
If I have a daughter,
I will iron her clothes long after she's old enough
to iron them herself.
I've never been good at housekeeping,
but I'm probably worse at advice,
except I can't seem to stop talking
to this empty space where,
just last month,
my uterus was.

III.
If I could have a daughter,
it would be my life goal to make sure she never—
not in a million years ever—
confused one kind of touch for another.
A woman has lost everything if she feels comforted
by the antibacterial caress of a man
who says if she gives it up now,
she'll havethe rest of her life
(so long as she can withstand the constant, hollow ring).

IV.

If I could have a daughter, I would implore her to enjoy philosophers and plumbers alike. On Prom Night, I wouldn't let her back inside the house until she told me about how her date couldn't get it up and so they'd made out half-naked and bewildered in his car until they got bored and smoked a joint. She could tell me they hadn't planned to use a condom, had planned to just see where things went and how far, but it wouldn't matter. She could tell me they'd almost run away together, just because. It wouldn't matter. *I have a daughter* is all that would matter.

"If I Have a Daughter" originally appeared in *Grain Magazine*.

Winter Solstice
by Mary Hennessy

*Couldn't this oldest of sufferings finally be for us more fruit-
ful?* —Rilke

Sometimes in the day, a distance opens
and you say, *I no longer get what I need*
and I say *I no longer have it to give.*

Sometimes in the day, a distance opens
and I realize that what you need most, I've lost—
the babies, the passports, the underlined copy of Proust.

Sometimes in the day, a distance opens
and a Renaissance angel walks in—
her face a featureless shelf

in front of careful curls—
both hands gone to what violence?
Do you see nothing?

And the day fills with crows—abrupt
and intimate in a manner
that shocks convention. Sometimes something sweeps

above or is it below, the dark water, troubling
it into a paler expression. *Do you know nothing?*
I know December.

I know the longest night is almost past.
Buds on the flame azalea swell in the dark
and we are turned in our turning
back towards the sun.

"Winter Solstice" originally appeared in *Indy Week*.

Statues

by Ed McManis

I read a poem about people
turning to stone. The idea's
not so new—it's in the Bible,
characters turned to pillars of salt

for doubting the Lord—

pay-back for the human itch
that makes you look
over your shoulder,
curse.

I remember people as trees
from my little sister's mythology
books with Middle Eastern
curlicue covers, and I recall her
gluing leaves to her arms
one summer, sticks in her golden
hair, how she stood next to the

giant elm out front, arms extended
in a "T" until she succumbed to
lunchtime and gravity.

Stone, salt, wood, I think
we secretly choose our elements
once we've squandered our life

force, waited in the wrong lines,
bled for the wrong people,
leaked our light.

I'm hoping for wings next, maybe
a griffin, even a stone lion,
something on horseback, though I

suspect the gargoyle rising
in my chest, nibbling on my heart
will consume me first.

Blackout
by JL Schneider

It's fitting that I sit
in the dark. I think this
and it's true, though it's too much

like being alone.
I should be with my wife
with the lights on

watching her fall
asleep. That's when she thinks
she can smell my intent.

After we make love
she reaches over in the darkness
and touches the corner of my eye

to see if I'm sad,
then my mouth
to see if I'm angry. Her finger

a roaming candle
lighting the lost participants'
secret features.

Object of Art
by Kate E. Schultz

They are, in a way, unaware
of my nakedness, making me
forget it too. Unashamed, I am Eve
before the fall, in this place
actually nothing like Eden, a place
where it's hard work to create beauty—
concrete floor spaces converted
into classrooms; industrial pipes
running the length of the ceiling.
What can I look at while they draw me,
paint me? Truly, here nothing is beautiful
in and of itself—I am just a collection
of parts, composition of muscle and bone
under skin. Their pencils skim paper;
the sides of their fists soften sharp lines.

It's day two of an extended five-class pose
and I can't remember which side my hair

was parted on for Tuesday's session.
One of the students sitting in front
of her easel wears men's swimming trunks—
turquoise printed with indigo sharks—
and black pseudo-combat boots, laces untied.
Her hair is shaved into a mohawk;
her eyes, winged with black liner. I'm curious to hear
the voice that belongs to this girl;
I wonder if I can make her face
abandon its deliberate lack of expression.
Before I walk to the mat and settle into my pose,
I ask her about my hair.

She looks at her canvas, then back at me,
saying, "I think the other side," in a voice
almost shy, a tone almost sweet,
and smiles. I don't think she knows
her mohawk and ill-fitting clothes don't disguise
her round cheeks, almost cherubic—like a baby's—
and flawless light skin. Her eyeliner
makes her long lashes stand out
even more. I've glanced at her many times
while she's worked, intent on representing
the truth, even though I heard
the professor say once:
"there is no truth—art is our own
subjective interpretation of reality,"
and although his self-consciously post-modern
declaration had made me want to roll my eyes,
now I see what he meant. I smile back at the girl
and adjust my hair with my fingers as I walk

to the mat, where I slip off my robe, lie back and fix
my gaze on the gray cement ceiling—its cracks
like lightning, pocks like stars.

"Object of Art" originally appeared in *Clementine Poetry Journal*.

Bundt Season
by DeAnna Stephens

Funerals one after another in summer-thin dresses. This one for a large man who touched his sisters when he was young and handsome. He would have liked me, but he's dead in the ground now, unsaved, they say, his heart exploded, so his widow deserves the pity, the yellow cake with a pound of margarine and half-dozen eggs. I convinced mother to leave it undone in the center, but doner than dough at the very heart because it's better that way. His son is the boy with the earring, the outcast at school who nods to me in the hallway but won't speak to anyone, and he'll be gone too, in a decade's time, and everyone who eats that cake, everyone for whom the cake was beaten and baked till not quite done. See the horrible headstone in the widow's yard. My mother says if she woke and looked at that every day ... She shakes her head. Lemon, always lemon because it is bright, clean on the palate, the opposite of grief.

How to Say Goodbye
by Neha Sud

The first-born son is meant to carry the casket,
but you have no siblings,
So, your father's body is your burden.

Hire three pallbearers to help,
You, buckling under the cadaver's weight,
They, stable,
as strangers who lend a shoulder often are.

Smell the breeze as it lifts sandalwood scent from the pyre.
Watch white muslin billow as you wrap it around the body,
leave only his feet protruding.
Lower the corpse onto stacked logs.

Notice that this is one of the few times
you've seen him lying upright.
As a child, you'd find him face down on the sofa,
cheek resting on your dead mother's photograph,
tears streaming.

Grasp a flaming log of wood.
Walk around the pyre counter-clockwise, three times,
Recite mantras.

Feel sweat pouring down your face.
Remember other sweltering walks:
a girl, walking home from school in summer,
backpack heavy,
reciting rhymes to forget that Dad didn't pick her up.
At home, she finds him sitting on the floor,
surrounded by her dead mother's things, staring, vacant.

Light these memories on fire along with the pyre.

As his flesh sizzles, picture the few times he saw you,
when he'd take you by the hand to the kitchen,
and fry up samosas in sizzling oil.
Briefly feel … not heat … warmth.
Mouth "I forgive you."

Collect his ashes,walk to the holy river.
Release them,
Watch his soul lift in the air, light, as he never was.

Now: walk away.
Feel how your feet don't quite touch the ground.

Jackie
by Elizabeth Vignali

3 am and awake because of the woman who called
and asked for Jackie. *You have the wrong number,*
I'd said, and hung up. I can't go back to sleep
because of the expectation in her voice, like
she was all jacked up on crying and had planned
out what she was going to say.
I want you back or *I'm finally leaving Joe*
or *How could you steal Joe from me?*

I listen to the train's wheels ringing down the tracks
by the water. I wonder if she got a hold of Jackie
or if she'd used up her determination with the wrong call.
Now she flicks the long column of ash from her cigarette
or now she lies next to Joe, her suitcase back in the closet,
or now she lies next to where Joe used to be
before he got drunk and kissed Jackie
at the company Christmas party.

When I was a kid, our phone number was one digit
different from the taxi company's. Every night
after the bars closed, drunks woke us with
their slurred requests, consonants running together

like smudged chalk. This was back when
there were still phone booths
and the scratched plastic-sheathed book
hanging on its heavy silver rope.
Dialing an 8 instead of a 3 was small
on the scale of mistakes one could make
depending on how one's evening was going.

Once when my mom answered the phone
the woman started crying. *This is my last quarter,*
she'd said. Mom put on her shiny white polyester robe
and drove downtown where the woman waited
outside the phone booth by the 3B tavern.
This was back when there were still phone booths
and the 3B and Mom. She drove the woman home.
She told her to always carry two quarters.

It's been an hour since the woman called for Jackie.
Now she slides her sore feet back
into her white nurse's shoes or now
she watches the fill and spill of Joe's sleeping breath
or now she finally falls asleep herself,
her hand buried between her thighs.
My mom wouldn't have hung up. *Tell me about Jackie,*
she would have said. I lie awake and listen to the silence
after the train, thinking about how I used to think
its whistle at night was the loneliest sound in the world.

"Jackie" originally appeared in *Natural Bridge.*

Morning Sickness
by Cady Vishniac

L isten: I eat it all
espresso grounds in my peanut butter
quail egg on salmon egg with a side of raw horse

but when I was knocked up
all food tasted like blood, even milk
chocolate and especially bread

I couldn't touch lasagna
or anything else in the world
there was a barrier

it was him, the way he looked at me
when I barfed in my kitchen
as if I had done something rude

I never worry about it much anymore
except the mother of his second child
told me *he thought it was my fault I was sick*

and I said *of course he did*
the injustice of it
my daughter and I photograph snails

and he is out there
we swing on a tire and he is out there
to spoil our joy; we bake blackberry muffins

in a silicone tin and he is out there
a hunter
I can take cream cheese and lox

and put it in an omelet
but I can't do a thing for the other women.

"Morning Sickness" originally appeared in *Tinderbox Poetry Journal.*

Three Drunk Angels
by Jeff Walt

Squat down in the cool shadow of a dumpster
behind Fat Jack's Tavern, sneaking
cigarettes, tips of their wings
dragging in puddles of urine and anti-freeze.
Souls are not arriving where they should.
Three drunk angels are sick of saving lives, sick of escorting
each delirious spirit from its hollow pod,
sick and tired of hanging out at 7-elevens waiting
for some nut with a gun to shoot the girl
behind the counter, then having to greet her
with a fake smile like a host
who wants the party to end. So they continue to inhale
long, deep hits, knowing all the while a baby is being
drowned
by his mother in a bathtub and his tiny melted soul
is even now running with soap scum down the drain.
Souls are not arriving where they should.
Souls sweep down the alley like ripped

plastic Foodland bags, stuck
to the bottoms of shoes. Souls are just another something
for the dog to bark at, about which the living ask,
"What is it boy, what's there, what do you see?"

Yellow Paper

by Amanda Kabak

Now that Kate was safely out of the way—silenced permanently in a corner plot with a view of the freeway—the pedigreed vultures swooped in. These scavengers of the literary community that had circled throughout her illness wanted her papers: rough drafts, outlines, sketches, and character studies, but mostly her letters. She left hundreds and hundreds of letters behind written in her quirky, tight hand, in her personal style, with her enchanting sense of humor. I had gotten my share of them over the years, so I knew exactly the object of their dried-up, academic love.

Despite the persistent wooing of her publisher, her alma mater, and one Professor Graham, who harbored an unhealthy professional infatuation, I avoided Kate's office during my slow progression of prying her things from our house. Admittedly, my delay in dismantling this last bastion of her was only partly to frustrate the academics. Mostly I knew that handling paper she had touched, that had touched her, was going to be exponentially harder than emptying her underwear drawer and confronting that half-eaten box of Wheaties just out of my short reach in the pantry.

To me, reading was heroin, a drug I mainlined at every opportunity and that transported me as surely as that poppy derivative. I read not only at normal times—in the tub, before bed, on my commute—but also while I brushed my teeth or scrambled eggs or walked to the grocery. Librarians knew me by name, and I'd once had to move to a bigger place to accommodate all my books. The most compelling proof of the existence of God is that I shacked up with a writer, and truthfully, my love for Kate just barely trumped my love for her words.

All of the thousands she'd left behind in her office tempted and scared me in equal measure. For months after the funeral, I was unable to cross the boundary of that long-closed door. Every time I eased down the hall past this tomb, I couldn't shake the image of Kate, sitting cross-legged in front of the bank of black file cabinets just inside, reorganizing for the umpteenth time, laying down playful posthumous commandments about the folders strewn about her.

"Don't let anyone in here, Audrey. If you have to, box it up and deliver it. Claim you were the one who put everything in order. Whatever. Better yet, just torch it."

All I could do was laugh. If I'd said anything, it was always something like, "Who are you kidding? You'll outlive us all."

But she didn't, and now I had to consider how much of what she said was real and how much was just the conflict between her inner compulsive and her public, bless-this-mess persona. She'd had years of illness during which to decide to bequeath them or destroy them, and she hadn't done either, so eventually, I had to choose for her. Kate's publisher forwarded proposals to me, and I sifted through them until one morning, I opened my front door to Walter Rosenberg, a no-name adjunct professor at a no-name college two hours away. I'd chosen him mostly because of the large upper hand it afforded me but also because of something he'd written in his dissertation on the modern Midwestern sensibility in literature: "Kate Harrison is subversive in how she approaches heavy topics like race and socioeconomics, laying them right at the surface of her prose without once interrupting the story underneath. Such a tactic is not the typical Midwestern one yet is extremely effective. To read one of Ms. Harrison's novels is to come out the other side exhilarated, amused, and forever altered." Forever altered. Yes.

Walter was impossibly young with an unkempt puff of light-brown, curly hair and a prominent Adam's apple.

"Walter," I said and shook his hand.

"Ms. Bishop. Thank you again for this opportunity." His eyes flicked past me to the foyer and beyond then back to my face, but I couldn't quite get myself to let him inside.

"I have rules."

He blinked, glanced up and down the block. "Okay…"

"First, no papers leave this house. Second, I retain the right to withhold anything we find. They were Kate's words, and now they're mine and everything that implies."

"Absolutely. I get it. I read through that agreement the lawyer put together. And Ms. Bishop, let me say—"

I held up my hand. "This is not about you or me but Kate. I believe in the power of her words. All of them. So

56

here we are, whether you need it or not, though I know you do, or whether you deserve it or not, which only time will tell."

Walter's serious earnestness slipped, revealing a grin that somehow made him look older. "Why do I feel like I'm trying to take your daughter out on a date?"

That was so much like something Kate would say that I came shockingly close to laughing. "All right. Come on."

I led him through the foyer and living room then down the hall, and when my hand landed on the knob of Kate's office door, I made myself turn it without hesitation. The cool air inside smelled like Kate before she got sick and turned sour like milk a day too old. At that scent and the sight of those filing cabinets, I knew this was still too soon. Then again, most mornings I still woke up thinking Kate was lying next to me.

Walter cleared his throat. "I meant to start out with my condolences for your loss. She was ... I saw her at a reading a few years ago, when I was finishing my dissertation. The way she told a story—and not just on paper but with her voice—she was a performer. She seemed like your cousin Ruth or something, the one your parents loved but told you to keep away from the wine."

"It was an act. At least partly. She was probably already sick then."

"I'm sorry."

I inhaled sharply. "The drawers and files are all labeled. Most people wanted to see her letters, but you were admirably vague in your proposal."

"That may be the first time those words have been used together in a complimentary way."

I wondered, briefly, why he didn't have a tenure-track position yet if he were this clever, but I just said, "Where would you like to start?"

"Um ... top left?"

The ice inside me melted a little at that. I opened the first drawer and tugged out a thick folder of yellow paper, which turned out to be a hand-written novel Kate had penned in college. We read it tag team with my passing each chapter to Walter after finishing it. The prose was so wonderfully awful compared to what I was used to from Kate that I laughed for the first time in a geologic age, imagining her writing it.

This exercise was going to take weeks. Months. And if this train wreck of a novel were any indication, I was going to fall in love with Kate all over again with each story. Even her bad writing brought her back to life in the same way she was conjured into existence whenever anyone opened a book she'd written. She hovered over your shoulder and spoke her words into your ear with her flat Midwestern accent, slapping you on the back over every good joke.

I remembered too well how Kate was at readings, especially the one at my local bookstore where we'd met. There she was on a random Tuesday after work, larger than life, so bright and bold and maybe a little too electrically *there* to be my type, but when she started to read, oh, I was mesmerized—not even by her words but by her vowels and consonants, even by the pauses between them.

When she finished reading, I picked a copy of her book off a tall stack and became the end of a line of people waiting for her signature. No one appeared after me, so we were alone when I arrived at her signing table. As a child, I'd had crushes on writers rather than rock stars, and I handed her the book with no small amount of trepidation, praying to God that her words would live up to her.

Her eyes were a warm brown and made her more approachable than her blunt-cut, chin-length hair and raucous laugh. A light spray of freckles decorated her cheeks, and I flushed so fiercely I all but shook with it. "That was a wonderful reading."

Kate's smile widened enough to dimple. "Thank you. I changed my mind about what to read at the last minute, so I wasn't sure how it'd go over. Do you know how many of my writer friends spend the remaining seconds before these things with their red pens out, editing right on the printed book? We're a mad bunch, I guess. Shouldn't be let out in public."

Yes, reading was my chosen drug, but Kate Harrison was the drug distilled and personified, and before I knew what I was doing, I'd offered my hand and introduced myself.

"Audrey," she repeated, took my book, and turned it over in her delicate fingers. "Do you drink coffee? Tea? Bourbon? I'm dying of thirst, and as wonderful as the staff is here, what do you say to sneaking out with me?"

Whenever the plot of my life twisted and bunched, I floundered around in stupefied indecision, and Kate must've mistaken this for serious hesitation. She looked embarrassed, her thin brows wrinkled. "I'm sorry. I shouldn't have. Here, let me sign this. I wasn't trying to hold it hostage or anything, I swear."

I found solid ground at her fluster and reached for the book. "Forget the signature, and let's get that drink."

Walter came over weekends and evenings—whenever I would let him and was around to supervise, though supervise probably wasn't the right word. Mostly, I didn't want to miss anything. Sometimes, while I pored over story drafts and character sketches, I even felt Kate's breath on my neck.

On the six-month anniversary of her death, Walter arrived, uninvited, holding flowers and a sympathy card, and I lost the rest of my reserve toward him. I'd woken up raw and angry and unbearably sad, and as much as I wanted to succumb to the pull of flannel and darkness and self-pity, I let him in. Instead of going back to Kate's office, we sat across from each other at the kitchen table, cupping our hands around mugs of hot coffee, dipping our faces toward their aromatic steam.

Without looking up, Walter said, "The first of her books I read was *Winter Wheat*, my freshman year in college. My professor was a raging feminist, so, you know. But the way that book worked on gender and lineage without *working* on them reminded me of Twain."

"Let's not talk about Kate."

"Everything we've been reading … don't they want to publish it?"

"She put them in the drawer for a reason, and not just because she was a pack rat. When she died, I found ten years of receipts in her sock drawer. *Ten years* of receipts for gifts she'd given me." I laughed, but it felt like glass in my throat. "Let's not talk about Kate."

The quiet that followed was dense and uncomfortable. Truth was that I very much wanted to talk about Kate or at least dip into those file cabinets. But what did Walter know about loss like this?

As if to prove my point, he said, "I've been applying for grants to pay for gas and some of my time doing this. I know you said there was a lot to go through, but you weren't kidding. I was thinking that maybe I'll try to get out of teaching one class this summer so I can focus more exclusively. I should be publishing as I go along, but who's got the time?"

I searched his face for a deeper meaning beyond this low-level whine. His unkempt stubble and fly-away hair had become familiar to me these past weeks, along with this wide-eyed boyish look, like each moment was surprising in some small way.

"Maybe if I could take some materials home with me. Just a folder at a time so I can start on the letters while we're still going through drafts here."

"No."

"I get it."

"No. No, you don't." My anger wasn't really anger but a slimy mix of fear, sadness, and fatigue. "You want her letters? Fine. Let's get to work, then." I left the kitchen and went to Kate's office, not waiting for him to follow, but when I opened the door and realized the air inside no longer smelled like her but, instead, of coffee and Walter's cologne, the grief of the day caught up with me.

"Audrey," Walter said from behind me. Maybe I should let him take the whole trove of words home, get it away from me, give me a fighting chance.

"Go home, Walter," I said without turning around.

"Do you mean—"

I sighed. "For today, Walter. Just for today."

*

Three or four months after Kate and I found each other, we endured a barrage of inquiries around when we were going to move in together, where we'd live, who was going to give up her lease, which neighborhoods we were considering. One night, when we were at our friends Tammy and Rachel's house, not long after they'd brought their new baby home, I had enough of the pestering. "What's the point of being a lesbian if you can't escape all these rules? I mean, Christ. What's the rush? Can't people just date anymore?"

Tammy, who'd known Kate the longest of all of us, shot a look across the table that spurred Kate into evidencing great interest in her asparagus. "Ah. You're dragging your feet."

Before she could confirm this terribly accurate assessment, the baby started crying in that short, alarmed way of newborns, his upset broadcast clearly through a monitor on the kitchen counter. Kate launched to her feet. "I'll get him," she said and slipped down the hall.

Tammy said, "I'm right, aren't I?"

I was distracted by the crying too much to lie. "Sometimes I think something's truly wrong with her. Like maybe emotional imbalance is required to be a writer. The way she can just completely disengage from the real world, be here and not at all here at the same time..."

"She's crazy about you."

"Or maybe just crazy?" I asked, half-seriously. The crying cut off as quickly as it had begun, and Tammy and Rachel sagged. I excused myself and went to find Kate, who sat in the nursery's rocking chair, her head bent toward the infant in her arms, whispering. Seeing her like this, quiet and almost small, removed any last doubt about wanting to be with her, *pledging* to be with her even if she never wrote another word. At this moment, I didn't care that she'd ever written a single word to begin with. "We need to talk," I said.

She put a finger to her lips then pointed at the baby monitor. I crept closer despite my historic unease around children under six, the age at which most of them could read and at least nominally reason. I knelt next to her and whispered, "I'm not on their side, but what's so wrong with wanting you around more?"

She turned to me with such quickness that the baby stirred and was set to start wailing again before she bounced it a few times and put the chair in motion. Speaking more to the baby than to me, she said, "But you seem so content when I'm not around."

"If you're not around, how would you know?"

"You know what I mean."

"No, actually, I don't."

"I'm only a little better than a mid-list writer; I've just been lucky."

"What does that have to do with anything?" It came out loudly, but I didn't care.

Kate shushed me. "It's just, a long time ago, I got invested like this but shouldn't have. I've learned how to be content enough, just like you are with your books. I know I'm not good at letting go. When I lost...," she shrugged and bent her head to the baby, her hair obscuring her face. "I lost a lot."

I wanted to strangle and kiss her, simultaneously. The memory of her tall and loud and vibrant behind the podium layered over her curled around that innocent baby caught between us, and I lost my senses in a rush of desire. "Books," I said, fiercely and loud, "are not enough. You think I haven't been hurt? Don't be stupid. But you love through it, despite it. What else is there?"

She brushed a finger against the baby's cheek, which looked as soft as it surely felt. When she finally turned to me, she was smiling in a crooked, sheepish, apologetic way that was so disarming she surely practiced in the mirror. "Nothing, Audrey. There's absolutely nothing."

*

Two months into this spelunking exploration of Kate's papers, out of loneliness or just plain insanity, I invited Walter to stay in our guest room. *My* guest room, I reminded myself. I told him I worried about him driving so much, which was true enough that I could ignore any more primary motives.

It turned out, though, that having someone else in the house made me think of Kate even more, her words becoming the centerpiece of every moment. Then we started in on her letters, and in a startling shift, the tower of Babel of her fiction fell away. While the recipients of her letters were spread across a wide range of locations, professions, backgrounds, and personalities, Kate's voice in them was always the same, as larger than life in the world of thought as she was in the physical one.

These folders hosted alternating processions of letters received—still in envelopes stuck with stamps of varying value—and copies of the letters she had sent out in response. Photocopies, computer printouts, hand-written duplicates on white scrap paper, smeared purple mimeographs. Even as she sent her words all over the globe, she couldn't bear to part with them.

I succumbed to the pull of Kate's voice, especially in dialogs that went beyond research into the personal, even taking them to bed with me to savor them well into the wee hours. In the next room, I could hear Walter typing hard on his laptop, the keys surely shying away from every stroke, and I knew that Kate was with both of us.

One Saturday, we sat in her office, sipping our morning coffee and reading, always reading, and I slid open the next file drawer in our exploration and saw it, a thick sheaf of yellow paper tucked, misfiled, between two folders. I froze. Kate never misfiled anything, and she used notepaper like this for first drafts only, never letters. She claimed to like how the color sometimes clashed with her ink, a result she called "an inspiring ugliness." But she never wrote first drafts for letters. And she never left papers misfiled.

I stood in indecision for so long that I felt Walter watching me. I turned my back to him and slid the papers free. The date at the top of the first page was years before we met. "I thought about you the other day," it started in a bright blue ink, "and I got angry out of sheer habit, furious at this weakness of mine, this problem of you I can't seem to solve like some tricky turn of phrase. Then I stopped, just like that, and I wondered what moronic asshole declared that thinking of someone so thoroughly lost was wrong.

"So, I decided to write to you … but not really. Even if the urge to send this captures me, the effort it would take to discover your address would be enough to put a halt to it.

It's a perfect arrangement. Safety tinged with the thought that you might someday, through some odd set of circumstances, actually read these words. I wonder what you'd think."

What was this? A letter, certainly, despite the lack of a name at the top, despite the color. I hefted the thick sheaf—equivalent in length to a short novel. Then, in a move I was sure had Kate turning in her grave, I flipped to the end. Although I was just looking for a date on the last letter, my eyes couldn't help but pick up a few phrases: "never leave me," "wish so much," "never had the opportunity." The date was almost exactly a month before she died.

Behind me, Walter shuffled pages with a sound as familiar as morning bird-song. I slid the stack of yellow paper into the nearest file folder of letters, tucked it under my arm, and took my usual position in an armchair in the corner I sometimes used to sit in when Kate worked in the evenings.

He said, "That's a big one. Who's it with?"

I looked at the label on the folder. "Marianne Deurault."

"Who's she?"

I shrugged. "Before my time."

"I still can't believe she wrote to Taylor Carpenter. The Yankees? An all-star shortstop? Listen to this: 'What I'd most like to know about are the currents that course through you when you're expecting a slider, low and outside, or when you notice a batter taking an open stance and drift to the right to cover the gap (I've absolutely seen you do this, and it's the height of impressiveness). When I get an idea, I sometimes mistake it for heartburn; it's an uncomfortable gnawing, a feeling of unresolvedness without anything as handy as a referent.' Really? Referent?"

"Yeah. Kate had a way with words."

He laughed.

"As, apparently, do I." I opened the folder in my lap, hiding the canary-yellow pages behind thick manila, and picked up where I left off.

"I have made you into a character as fictional as my own but more dear to me—if that's possible. I know very well it isn't to you that I write but instead to my idea of you, but I can't help but wonder how far from the truth that idea is. It comforts me to think that I know you."

I got sucked into these letters as quickly as into one of Kate's novels. Though they were spaced months apart, they had the feel of an irrepressible blurt. Kate had apparently met this person in college when she was just twenty, though she didn't detail the circumstances. Kate at twenty was a thought I had to caress for a long while before I could put it aside. She'd seemed so very herself at forty, when I'd first set eyes on her, that it was strange to imagine her with only half those years, no streaks of gray, a tighter and sleeker body, and no laugh lines around her eyes and mouth.

A couple dozen letters in, I appeared on the page. "I've met someone. Zing. I felt it, and it surprised me and then scared me half-to-death. I jumped in, braving loss and traumatic repercussions, but now here I am, scratching out this letter because you have invaded my mind like an avenging angel. What am I going to do with you? How am I going to tell Audrey?"

I remembered the night Kate "jumped in," a month after that dinner at Tammy and Rachel's. She showed up at my door, flushed and smiling, dark hair windblown. She hovered just outside the threshold, said she felt twenty again, then in a move steeped in atypical shyness, offered up a ring—the same one still welded to my finger. I yanked her inside, and the kiss that followed, searing and final, was one of my most precious memories.

Twenty again. The reality of these letters, what they meant to Kate for all those years, began to sink in. I weighed the stack still in my hands then riffed through it. When I glanced up at Walter, he was watching me, and I felt like I'd just woken from a book five bus stops past my destination, other passengers staring. Oh, I was caught—on so many levels, too. Not only with these letters but also with my abandonment of getting beyond Kate's death in any way. Just like she couldn't get beyond this lost love?

I couldn't think about that. Not now, not with Walter watching. As if to underscore his scrutiny, he asked, "Are you okay?"

I closed the folder, trying to minimize its existence. "I'm … I need some air, I think. I shouldn't be here," I added before I could stop myself, but it was true. These letters in my hands were one thing, but hanging on to a ghost like I was doing? "I need some air," I repeated, but instead of opening a window, I disappeared to our bedroom (*my* bedroom) and tucked the papers in the drawer of my nightstand.

Then I hurried to the front door, desperate to escape this futility of grief. I kept my foot on the gas until, after a long, meandering route, I was in a random small town, sitting in a corner of its public library, reading Hemmingway with an unbecoming desperation. He was the writer perhaps the most unlike Kate. Spare, masculine, deadpan. I longed for him to spirit me from my life in a way he'd never managed to before, and he failed me again this time.

This was not at all what Kate would want. She'd said it in so many words at each of our anniversaries. "You do realize that I've ruined you forever for a life of the mind. Once you've loved like this, you'll never be happy with just books again." What she'd neglected to mention was the high likelihood that no one else could ever come close to filling her size-ten shoes. She'd scoff at that, but the reality was that I might live another twenty years without her, and though I very clearly still couldn't conceive of her permanent absence, I knew without a doubt that I'd love and miss her until my last breath.

Clearly I had to get all those papers out of the house. After that, if loneliness and heartbreak had their way with me and left me still alive, which was what was purported to happen, I would decide about the rest of my life then.

When I got back, the house was silent as a grave, not even broken by the hum of the refrigerator. It even felt darker than usual. I stood in the foyer for a moment, letting my eyes and ears adjust. "Walter?" I called even though I didn't remember seeing his car at the curb. He was out, blowing off steam like I always told him to do, but even as I thought that, I navigated the dark hallway to Kate's office. I turned on the light and saw a short stack of paper on the desk with a note sitting on top. I was drawn to it with a cracking, dreadful inevitability.

Of course it was those letters—it couldn't but had to be at the same time. I snatched the note off the top before confirming my suspicions. It read: "Audrey, I'm not sure if you'll hate me or ultimately thank me for what I've done."

I stopped reading and levitated to the file cabinets, yanking open each drawer in turn. By the time I'd peered into the empty, black depths of each, I was shaking and breathing hard, making noises that didn't resemble sounds I was even physically capable of producing.

I lurched back to the desk and willed my eyes to focus on the note, to decipher Walter's scratchy cursive. "Not long after I started here, I paid a lawyer to look over our agreement, and while you could seize the writing from me, I'm still allowed full access, including copies. Maybe you can be a little happy to have enabled a career for me—and ultimately let readers know the real Kate.

"I can see you tried to hide these from me for good reason. I doubt you made it all the way to the end earlier today, but you were right as to their importance. I feel I owe you the originals, but I took copies. Fantastic!

"Thank you from the bottom of my thieving heart. Walter."

My brain wasn't functioning correctly, fizzed and popped around words and visions and emotions, leaving me only enough solidly connected synapses to wonder if I were having a stroke. I collapsed into Kate's chair, yelled, "Motherfucker!" then clapped a hand over my mouth.

Through the shocked static in my mind, I wondered why Walter mentioned the end of these letters. They weren't a book. There was no plot, no pending resolution outside of Kate's death, but his words bothered me enough to thumb through the stack to where I'd left off, to Kate's proposal, and start in again.

I appeared on these yellow pages on and off over the years—always with love, but always, *always*, with the mention of the secret she kept of this communication. "I wonder so much what you and Audrey think about me. You more than Aud because she's here to ask in the wee hours of the morning when my self-assurance wanes like my metabolism. But even then, I'm all-too aware of the things I haven't told her. You, for example. What would she think of me if she knew about you—not just the past but this strange sort of present I force into existence?

"And you, I wonder what you would think if you could read these letters and know that I have always continued to hold you in my heart as I suspected I would."

In these letters, I saw story and novel ideas take hold and get fleshed out, skimmed over whole paragraphs of essays she'd later published, and wondered what came first, the letter or the "real" first draft. Later, I relived those years when Kate became ill and realized she wasn't going to bounce back. While her handwriting proceeded unchanged, her tone was subtly altered, and it made me hurt all over again, remembering her slow but steady decline. She wrote as much as she could but was often frustrated by physical fatigue affecting her mental prowess.

I remembered the day I understood that she had resigned herself to death. We were sitting across the kitchen table from each other, and out of the blue and in a way that stopped any thought of further conversation, she said, "I think I'm going to stick to short stories from now on. Maybe even poetry." I excused myself as quickly as I could without being obvious, went to the bathroom, turned on the taps, and cried until my head pounded.

Then the last letter. I didn't want to read it, wanted to save these words to know there would always be more of Kate still left to learn, but I was a reader as much as Kate's wife, and I had never, not once, stopped this close to the end. I promised myself to go slowly.

"Even after all these years, I still haven't explained, have I? Maybe you were never told that you were adopted, that someone, *me*, had given you up mere minutes after bringing you into the world. But you were, and I did, and my darling boy who I've never known, I still don't know what to think about that."

My ears roared. Literally. They were filled with a rolling white noise, and my assaulted mind could not be stopped from thinking that I'd always scoffed at that description in books, always considered it a lazy cliché, but it was absolutely true.

A baby? A boy? Kate had mentioned she'd been with men when she was young and stupid—hadn't most of us?—but a baby? A boy?

I read on, gulping down the words. "Your father was at least partly right. Keeping you would have been a mistake—maybe not the disaster he predicted and certainly harder than I imagined—but I still couldn't conceive of aborting you. *Our* child? A child of love? Because I did love him. Enough to lose my senses at least a little.

"At the hospital, your new parents were waiting. I could feel them around the ragged edges of pain and sadness and grief and a thousand other things. They were there, and he wasn't, and all I could do with that was breathe and push and breathe again, whatever the nurse told me to do, whatever the doctor asked. While the labor progressed, I made sure everyone knew I didn't want to hold you or see you. I didn't want to change my mind. Couldn't. Probably wouldn't, but I couldn't risk it.

"Eventually, you cried, and I cried, and I found that I had to know, so I asked, and they told me, and you were a boy. A healthy boy who is now 42, if nothing terrible has happened, who has lived a life I have no way of imagining, let alone knowing.

"All this time, all these words between then and now, and I've never once written of it, not even written close to it. These letters to you, this graven image of you I've been directing these words to, this muse I've made you into—let's be honest. I eventually forgave your father, even forgave myself, but you will never leave me, not that I want you to. I keep you close, secret, so that you can't escape despite how I let you go, so that I can keep you safe in a way I never had the opportunity to.

"I wish so much that I could have known you."

I put the letter down and cried like I hadn't since the night after she'd died, when the relief of her being past her suffering and the numbness of shock both wore off. I was so wretched and thorough in my sorrow that I slid from the chair and was huddled half under Kate's desk by the time I calmed. My chest ached, and I was afraid to move, knowing the contraction of muscle would shake loose thoughts I wasn't sure I wanted to think.

I rotated my wrist just enough to see my watch—nearly two in the morning—and that was enough. Why hadn't she told me? Did she not trust me? Was she ashamed? She didn't sound ashamed. Resigned, maybe. Sad but not really regretful, not about giving up her son and not about keeping this from me.

The betrayal of this secret made me feel, finally and completely, the betrayal of her illness and subsequent death, of her leaving me too young after too little time together. Then, not only leaving me like that but leaving me with *this*. In my anger, I got up to find Walter, to spew vitriol at someone who might have the vaguest possibility of understanding, and I remembered the empty drawers and the jocular note. There they went again, my ears, and in their din, I imagined Walter's first article, the follow-on book, a tour that could wash me up at his signing table where I'd bash his teeth in.

I was shaking, punch drunk, ears not roaring anymore but ringing in the heavy cotton batting of quiet in the house. Yet just to the side of my stunned fury was a resonance of loss, and I thought I could feel a little of what Kate had felt in that delivery room, an emptiness terrible and final, an acceptance of facts long gone unacknowledged in just this way.

I hated so much that Walter knew this about Kate before I did. But, even more, I hated that I never had the chance to hear her talk about this directly, to let her lean on me in memory. I hated that Kate didn't have the courage to expose this old hurt. She played the big-boned gal with the corn twang perfectly, but the only way she could tell me about this was by leaving these words to be found by whoever came along.

She was well and truly gone to me just like her son had always been well and truly gone to her. All I had left that I could put my hands on was this stack of yellow paper. I weighed the sheets in my hands, wanting so much to make my own idol of them, to imbue them with a Kate still somehow alive. It would be so easy to slide them back in the drawer of my nightstand, read a page every night, and go to sleep with Kate still curled around me.

Instead, I got up and went to the living-room fireplace. I tossed the papers onto the hearth, fished out a long match, and struck it against the stone. I sat for a minute working up the nerve, the flame devouring the match little by little. But when the corner of the stack curled up and blackened, my heart seized. I lunged in to grab the papers, and my hand jerked back, singed.

Then, just as I was going to cry, I started to laugh, instead. Christ, Kate, what an unbelievable mess you've made, keeping this to yourself for so long only for it to escape so completely. She'd managed to let go of it, somehow, releasing these singed and curling pages to fate, Walter's hard drive, and our fireplace, and all that was left for me to do was the same. Let her go. Watch this part of her burn and find some kind of freedom in it.

Cry on Command
by Joe Dornich

Somber, graceful mourning, with maybe the occasional tear or two, that's one hundred. We call it a Dry. Hysterical crying, with the wailing and the moaning and the classic rhetorical questions screamed to the heavens—the *How could you*'s, the *Why now*'s—that's going to cost you two-fifty. We call those, and really any tear-related mourning, a Wet. Some weeks Feldman will assign me nothing but Dries. Others, it will be one Wet after another. Those weeks can be exhausting.

Occasionally we'll get a client that requests the "Grecian Widow." They want to see me insane with grief, destroyed by loss, throwing myself on the casket and threating to jump into the grave. Those can run upwards of five hundred.

Not that I get anything close to that. What I get is ten to fifty dollars a funeral plus tips. Not that anyone tips. You'd think Feldman would at least reimburse me for expenses. Like the mascara I go through after a week of Wets. Like my dry cleaning. *Black doesn't show stains,* he likes to remind me, and yes, generally it doesn't. But when you're crawling through freshly turned earth in a dress already damp with tears, it tends to leave a mark.

The only expense Feldman covers are the forget-me-nots I lay on each casket before it's lowered in the ground. Forget-me-nots, of course, being the official flower of the professional mourner.

Monday I get to the office five minutes late, but just in time to get nearly tackled by some woman reeling through the lobby. She's young, maybe half my age, and pretty, though it's hard to tell with the wide-eyed look of panic on her face.

"What's with her?" I ask Evelyn, our Receptionist and Bookings Coordinator.

"Failed the Fish Test."

I look again at the woman. She's wearing black heels and a matching, sleeveless dress. The dress still has the tags on it.

Of course.

The Fish Test.

Potential mourners-for-hire don't come in to interview so much as audition. After making them stew in the lobby for a few minutes, Feldman invites them into his office. On his desk is a small fish tank. It's a nice tank. It has colored rocks and a plant. It has one of those little treasure chests that periodically burps out bubbles. And, swimming inside, it has a solitary clown fish.

"This is Nemo," Feldman tells them.

"Like from that movie?" they say.

"Like from that movie," Feldman says.

The fish's name is an obvious and intentional reference. People get it and it makes them feel intelligent. Confident. They smile. They relax a little. In some small way a bond is formed. This is key.

"Can you cry on command?" Feldman says.

This question comes right from our ad. At the bottom, in bold letters it reads: THOSE THAT CANNOT CRY ON COMMAND NEED NOT APPLY.

They say yes. Every applicant says yes.

Feldman says let's see. Then he reaches into the tank and grabs the fish. "Follow me," he tells them.

They walk into the bathroom.

"Welcome to Nemo's funeral," Feldman says. "You're distraught. Overcome with grief. Let me see it. Lay it on me." Then he drops Nemo into the toilet. Both watch as Nemo swims a few disoriented laps around the bowl. Then Feldman flushes.

Almost everyone fails. I suppose it's the spontaneity or shock of it all. It's too much. People freeze up.

Most people.

"If you can't cry for this fish," Feldman says, "this fish who, less than a minute ago embodied the inane reference you so valued, then how can you possibly cry for a complete stranger?"

It's a fair question.

It's at that point most people grab their things and go.

What they don't know, not that it would help them with their grief problem, is that the toilet's a prop. It's not connected to the sewer. Nemo, the water, all come out of a pipe on the other side of the wall and empty into a bucket. On average, Nemo "dies" four to five times a week.

When I first started working here some of the other employees were quick to praise Feldman's humanity, his respect for God's creatures. But Feldman doesn't kill the fish because he's a humane animal lover. Feldman doesn't kill the fish because he's a cheap bastard.

The woman in black is still outside of our lobby. She's hunched over by the bushes and crying now. Sobbing really. It's a messy, mucus-heavy type of crying. Every few seconds she wipes her face, and then wipes her hands on her dress.

She better be careful or the store won't take it back.

"Sure," Feldman says, walking over, Nemo's bucket sloshing in his hand, "now she can cry. What a waste. Nothing worse than seeing a woman cry for free."

When Feldman first started this business it was simply about addressing attendance concerns. Maybe the deceased was new to the area and hadn't made a lot of friends. Maybe their relatives were far away, or in some cases, no longer living. Either way a low turnout was expected, and nobody wants a poorly attended funeral.

But soon word got around. Soon it became about more than just attendance. People realized they could transfer their grief. They could hire someone to provide the requisite amount of sadness and suffering while maintaining their composure. Their refinement. Because when someone dies, the human custom and social obligation to mourn their loss still exists, but for those at a certain tax bracket, there's a level of grieving that is, apparently, unbecoming.

That's where we come in.

Feldman likes to remind us that we're more than professional mourners; we're grief surrogates. That through us, people are able display their loss. Through us, they're able to pay their respects.

But sometimes I'm not so sure. Sometimes I think I'm perpetuating this myth that people can be insulated from loss, from sadness. Sometimes I think I'm just another way for them to avoid reality.

According to my schedule, I have two Dries and four Wets this week, beginning with a Level III Wet this afternoon. Technically, a Level III is "high-pitched, stuttering sobs with continuous tears," but around the office we call it Chipmunk Crying.

It costs one seventy-five.

The deceased is a Mr. Miles Hoglund, the former President and CEO of something called Hog-Smart Industries. It makes me think of a bunch of pigs in lab coats staring intently into microscopes, though that's probably not accurate.

His service is well attended, which suggests that he was popular with his employees, or that attendance was mandatory.

I'm situated off to the side, next the casket and a large photo of Mr. Hoglund on an easel. In it he has thick, silver hair and bushy eyebrows. A playful smile. He looks like he was a kind man.

After everyone has settled in, a priest reads a few passages from the Bible. Then he tells us not to mourn for Mr. Hoglund, that he is spending eternity living in the house of the Lord. He tells us our job is to continue to find glory and salvation here, the land of the living.

As he talks, I watch a bird peck at a malt liquor bottle someone has dumped in the weeds growing around a crooked tombstone.

The priest finishes, and then a man stands and addresses the crowd. He's tall and lean and emits a health club glow. His cologne is penetrating.

"Today we say goodbye to a great man. A pillar of the community and the bedrock of our work family. To me, and I'm sure you'll all agree, Mr. Hoglund wasn't just a boss he was a mentor. A father figure really. Because doesn't a father protect and provide for his family? That was Mr. H to a tee. Remember when we had that spat of break-ins and muggings in the common lot of employee parking? Who was it that made sure each and every one of you got a pepper-spray keychain in your stocking at the Christmas party? Even Stephanie Goldfarb got one, didn't you? Where are you Steph?

Everyone turns in their plastic folding chairs as a woman in a black cardigan slowly raises her hand while lowering her head.

"You weren't overlooked or forgotten just because you don't believe in Christmas. And why was that? Because Mr. Hoglund didn't discriminate. And he listened. Like a good father, Mr. Hoglund listened to his family. When we had a few rough quarters and the austerity measures began to take hold, who heard your concerns? Who, in less than three months time, reinstituted complimentary toilet paper in almost every restroom? You know, every day I took comfort in the knowledge that Mr. Hoglund was up on thirty-three protecting us, and listening to us. Watching over us. And he still is. He's still up there. Sure, he's up a little higher now, probably playing golf with Reagan, but he's still there. Mr. Hoglund is still there for you. Now, like then, his door is always open. Except now of course you don't have to make an appointment and have Margery escort you on to the executive elevator. So now as we undergo a transition, and I attempt to fill some very large shoes, I want all of you to still feel free to talk to Mr. Hoglund. Discuss your concerns. Share your problems. Try to keep these talks brief, or even better, save them until you've clocked out, but still, don't feel that you have to come to *me* with every little issue. Maybe, instead, allow Mr. H to continue to be the father of our work family. Our father, in heaven. Now let's all give him a big hand."

Then everyone applauds.

Everyone but me.

I just cry.

When people hear about my job the first things they ask are, *how do you do it? How do you cry on command? And so easily? Do you think of sad things?* And sure, some of us do. Some mourners maintain a mental catalogue of sad images. A three-legged puppy. An orphan with a lisp. An orphan, who upon being asked if they'd like a puppy, regardless of the missing leg issue, responds with an overjoyed, *Yes pwease!*

Everyone has their triggers. The important thing is to find what works for you.

Other mourners rely on performance enhancement techniques. They'll rub dish soap in their eyes. Hide bits of raw onion in their handkerchiefs. Some pinch themselves through their dress. Others pluck out a nose hair or two.

Me, I just think about the fact that I'm a fifty-year-old widow, that late my husband had been lying to me for the majority of our marriage, and now, because of that, our business and savings are gone, and my job is to cry at strangers' funerals.

I think of that and I have no problem crying.

The day my husband died he was attending a groundbreaking ceremony for our second restaurant. Just after he and some of the other investors put on the matching hardhats, and stuck their shovels into the ground, and smiled for the camera, Gene collapsed. He had a heart attack. They said he was dead within minutes.

A few weeks later a young man called asking if I'd like a copy of the photo. The photo of my husband right before he died? Who would want such a thing? I was furious. I called that young man some names I now regret.

Then I called back and asked him to please send me the picture.

I still haven't been able to look at it.

Gene and I met almost twenty years ago. On our first date he told me his dream was to start a business combining the two great loves of his life. I used to think that at some point I made it to the top of that list, but those first two: Catholicism and Chinese food.

Gene told me he experienced it for the first time while vacationing in San Francisco. He was in some hot and crowded dive in a back alley of the Tenderloin, and after that first mouthful, he was hooked.

Chinese food that is. Not Catholicism.

I've tried here and there to get into it, but I never really developed a taste for it. I think part of the problem's that it was forced upon me as child.

Catholicism that is. Not Chinese food.

But Gene was so passionate, so determined. His enthusiasm was infectious, and truth be told, I was falling in love.

So I agreed to help.

Gene and I worked hard, and we saved, and nine years later we opened our first Wok With Jesus.

Our first, and now it seems, our last. Things have been difficult since Gene passed. I've missed the last two mortgage payments and now the bank is talking foreclosure and has started repossessing assets. I tried increasing revenue. I tried coupons and circulars. I tried a deal where kids eat free on Wednesdays. We had some dedicated customers from the church, but then Burton Hoover, our day manager, was arrested. By the FBI. It seems that between greeting customers and politely inquiring if they were "right with the Lord"—a practice I never endorsed—and wishing them a "blessed day" on their way out, he was slowly filling the office computer's hard drive with child pornography. The FBI confiscated the computer and ordered the store closed pending an investigation.

So the church people are gone, and the investors have pulled out, and any hopes of revenue are a moot point.

I'm halfway home from the Hoglund funeral when I realize tonight's my turn to make dinner. I stop off at the restaurant to heat up a few things. Might as well use what's left before it goes bad. Before the bank takes the rest of it.

We're down to our last wok, and the gas company has cut us off, so I'm forced to use some Sterno cans to cook the food. Needless to say it's slow going. I wander around the restaurant to pass the time.

I imagine when the bank takes over and this place eventually becomes another Walgreens or Starbucks, the first thing they'll do is paint over the mural.

Before our grand opening Gene commissioned a local artist to paint a mural of Jesus between the two buffet stations. The artist rendered Him in the style of The Last Supper—arms out, palms up—as if to indicate the varied and bountiful array of Chinese delicacies. Or so I assume. Gene loved it, but I've always thought something wasn't quite right. It's the face. The lips are too pursed, and the eyes are too narrow, and the whole thing gives off an impression of judgment. As if He knows our General Tso's chicken is more breading than meat. Or that our egg drop soup comes from a mix. And sure, that's all true, but to me, it's easy to pass judgment when one doesn't have to deal with rising food costs. Not all of us can take a few fish and some bread and feed the masses.

Gene wanted to have the artist come back later and add some scripture. Something relevant. Something about ye eating and drinking in the glory of the Lord. But he never did. I talked him out of it. I thought it was an unnecessary expense and, ultimately, we put the money towards a soft-serve ice cream machine.

The bank took the ice cream machine last Friday.

When the food is cooked I box it up, and then take one last look around. The desk in the office looks so much bigger without the computer. Hanging on the wall is the first dollar we made. Gene had it framed. On the bottom is a plaque with the date, and this inscription: *The realization of a dream. The support of a best friend.*

I take the frame from the wall, break the glass on a corner of the desk, and shove the dollar into my purse.

Goddamn you Gene.

When I get home it takes me another ten minutes to find parking because I have to park in the street. Because there's a Windstar in my driveway. The Windstar belongs to my sister Constance and her husband. It's their RV. I'm sure in its day the Windstar was the height of recreational travel technology, but it's long past its prime. Like a lot of us. It's once gold paint has suffered decades of sun bleaching, and now it more closely resembles the color of unbrushed teeth.

Connie and Warren were in the middle of crisscrossing America when Gene died, so they postponed their trip to attend the service and help out. They've been here ever since. I know they're ready to get back on the road, and part of me is ready for them to go, but I also know Connie is worried about leaving me alone.

Truth be told, I'm a little worried about being left alone.

Neither of us knows what to do, and we're not really talking about it, so until then the Windstar's hulking, leaking mass will continue to sit in my driveway, its back end blocking the sidewalk, its right side tires ruining my lawn.

Connie meets me at the front door. She's wearing another one of her T-shirts. At some point Connie's entire wardrobe has been replaced by souvenir T-shirts from the various stops of their trip. Yesterday's shirt featured an anthropomorphic cowboy hat warning me not to "Mess with Texas." Tonight it's one from their Mount Rushmore trip, with a picture of the monument emblazoned across her chest.

Connie's husband is already seated at the dining room table.

"How are you Warren?"

"Hungry."

"Well, dinner's right here," I say, holding up the take-out boxes.

"Chinese food. What a surprise."

We spend the first few minutes eating in relative silence, the room filling with the clinking of silverware, and the way Warren chews his food so that everything sounds crunchy regardless of its consistency.

"Have either of you talked to Mindy lately?" I say.

Warren grunts out a lungful of air, and throws his fork to his plate where it plops in a pile of shrimp lo mein with little dramatic effect.

"Did I say something wrong?"

"No," Connie says. "It's just Mindy's new job. It's got Warren a touch perturbed."

"My daughter's selling her body like a common whore," he says.

"Warren, she is not," Connie says.

"She lays with strange men."

"She snuggles them," Connie reminds him, and then to me says, "She's cuddling people. It's a healing practice. Oriental I think. They say it's very therapeutic. Plus, it's certified."

"It's for the best you and Gene couldn't have kids," Warren says.

Actually it wasn't so much we couldn't, as we just didn't. There was always the restaurant to think of, and concerns about money. Time got away from us and we just never did. Then at some point, we changed *didn't* to *couldn't*. We both knew it wasn't true, but somehow it made us feel better. I've never told Connie that and I'm sure as hell not telling Warren now.

"Because kids will break your heart," he continues. "Sure, they start off as your little angel, as Daddy's little girl, but before you know it they're all grown up, and then they spread their legs and fly away."

"Oh my," Connie says, putting a hand to her chest, covering Roosevelt and half of Jefferson. "Darling, I think you mean wings."

"What?"

"Wings. They spread their wings and fly away."

"No. I don't. Idiot."

Then Warren stands, grabs his plate, and informs us that he'll be in the Windstar. When he's gone I ask Connie if she remembers Tammy Newton from high school.

"No, I don't believe so."

"Sure you do," I say. "Tammy Newton. She was in Ms. Marr's Algebra class with us. Red head. Sort of a heavy-set girl."

Connie shrugs with her face.

"She was always eating *those* cookies, and telling everyone how her great-grandfather founded the company. All of the kids called her Pig Newton."

"Sorry," Connie says. "It doesn't ring a bell. What about her?"

"She's dead. I'm working her funeral on Saturday."

After dinner I head upstairs and lie down. I watch some TV. The Monday Night Movie is some awful remake of *Citizen Kane* where the title character is even more bloated than in the original, and, for some reason, Scottish.

I change the channel. I change the channel and there he is—standing before a pulpit with his two-tone pompadour and ridiculous goatee, his fat face contorted into a mask of sanctimony—Roland Ravanel.

Ravanel is one of the more successful televangelists preaching something called the Prosperity Gospel, which centers on the concept of Seed Faith. Practitioners of Seed Faith believe they can sew seeds, which symbolize their belief and devotion to God, which, in turn, increases the power of His love, and likelihood He'll answers their prayers.

Even now, Ravanel is pounding a fist to the pulpit, imploring his followers to increase the amount of their seeds, so when their inevitable harvest comes in, it will be all the more miraculous. Then the camera pans over to a giant, stained glass eagle, it's wings spread, a golden cross in its talons.

Of course "seeds" mean money, and "sewing them" means sending that money to Ravanel's church, and the only miracle is that Gene had been doing this for the last twelve years and I had no idea.

I found out after he died. Gene handled all of the finances—the mortgages, the bills here, the books for the restaurant—all of them. Then when I took over, I learned he'd given away almost everything we had.

I remember in the days following Gene's funeral, being paralyzed at the thought of having to go through his things and the memories and pain they'd trigger, and how, in an instant, I went from that, to ripping his jackets and suits from their hangers, and dumping out his dresser drawers.

That's how I found the letters. In shoe boxes beneath Gene's side of the bed were hundreds of letters. All of them from Pastor Roland Ravanel and his Garden of Faith Ministry. All of them congratulating Gene on his devotion, confirming his ever-growing place in God's heart, and compelling him to send more. All of them addressed to a post office box I had never heard of.

I called the Ministry demanding to speak to someone in charge, demanding some answers. I was transferred four times and made to listen to over an hour's worth of upbeat, Christian hold Muzak. Then Ravanel himself came on the line. He told me that Gene's contributions were of his own volition. That it was all perfectly legal. Then he said the amount of seed Gene had sewn over the years had been considerable, and he was undoubtedly enjoying a glorious place in heaven beside the Lord. He said this, I suppose, thinking it would make me feel better.

It did not.

Then Ravanel wished me a "blessed day" and hung up. That's how Connie found me—the bedroom torn upside down, Gene's things scattered everywhere, and me sitting in the middle of the floor, crying, and screaming at the phone. She sat down with me, wrapped her arms around my shoulders, dried my face on her T-shirt.

It told me that, "Everything's Peachy in Georgia."

Now Ravanel, microphone in hand, is pacing the electric blue carpet of his stage. He's asking his followers if they're lost, and in pain, and desperate for relief. "Wouldn't you like to know that these sorrows and struggles aren't yours alone to carry?" he says.

The show cuts to members of the audience crying and nodding their heads.

Then Ravanel starts crying too. His expression morphs into a doughy swell of pity, and manufactured tears leak from his beady, black eyes.

But it's not real. He's just aping their grief. He's just capitalizing on their needs, and the hollow promise he can take their pain away.

I spend the rest of the night lying awake, trying to convince myself that Ravanel and I are not one in the same. That our roles, our intentions are different. But I can't. The similarities are too numerous, too painfully obvious. Accepting it is only a matter of time.

It doesn't mean it makes me feel better.

First thing Tuesday morning is a pet funeral. Our rates for an animal service are the same as a human's. Our price point depends on the degree of mourning, the amount of physicality in our grief, not what's in the box. Most animal service clients request a standard Dry, or maybe a Level I Wet – silent, yet streaming tears – but what they really want is some company. As they say their final goodbye to what is likely the last companion they had in the world, they simply don't want to be alone.

Some of the other mourners complain when Feldman assigns them a pet funeral. They think it's beneath them. But not me. I don't mind. The way I see it, these animals were loved as much, and were a part of these people's lives just like any other family member. In some cases, even more so. Plus I've always found it easier to cry for animals than for people.

When I get back to the office I see Evelyn crying at her desk. At first I think she is considering some work in the field, and maybe practicing her technique. But no. Her grief is real. As she collects her things and puts them in a box, Evelyn tells me she made a mistake with the anniversary mailers.

For an extra twelve dollars we'll send a remembrance card on the anniversary of a loved one's passing. Evelyn says that in our latest mail out there was a bit of a mix-up. It seems she accidently sent the card intended for the family of Bentley Morris, a golden retriever, to the former home of Bradley Morris, the deceased son of Craig and Susan Morris. I say that doesn't sound so bad. Then Evelyn tells me that Bradley was severely epileptic and died of a grand mal seizure. Then she hands me a copy of the card. It reads: *On this day know that your little Bradley is in Heaven, thinking about you, and wagging his tail.*

Evelyn says Feldman has discontinued the service, and to absorb the revenue loss, he's letting her go. I know she's struggling. Not only is she raising two little girls on her own, but the younger one has some sort of foot issue—no arch, or too much of an arch, I forget which—and has to limp around in a corrective boot.

I march down to Feldman's office but he doesn't want to hear it. He says Susan Morris is some bigwig on the Chamber of Commerce and the word of mouth alone could ruin us. He says an example needs to be made. He says it's out of his hands.

Still, I continue to protest, but Feldman waves a Client File in my face.

"I know you're upset," he says. "Good. Go use it."

Then he hands me the file and tells me not be late.

It's another rich guy's funeral. Late sixties. Millions in the bank. Died on his catamaran. His four kids from his three marriages are here, but neither of them looks too bereaved about Dad's death. Honestly, they seem a bit bored. The current wife is here as well, though she looks young enough to be one of the kids.

A trophy-wife client always makes for a difficult job. They still want someone else to do the messy work of grieving, but they don't want to be overshadowed, or outmourned.

Like this one. Even though the wife requested and paid for a Level III Wet, throughout the service she keeps giving me this look. She keeps narrowing her eyes and furrowing her otherwise unlined face as if to say, *Hey, reign it in a little.*

So I reign it in a little. I give her what she wants. I know my place. I may appear to mourn for the dead, but I cry for the living.

The thing about being a professional mourner is that the job is almost entirely physical, and, over time, that physicality becomes habitual. Muscle memory takes over. It allows the mind to wander.

I think about the people that send Ravanel money, the people that attend his services. Almost all of them are extremely ill, or the loved ones of an ill person. They're hoping to be saved from Parkinson's, or have their paralysis cured, or be free from cancer. They're hoping for a miracle. But not Gene. Gene wasn't sick. Even his heart attack came as a surprise to his doctor. So what was it? What was it about our life that he was so desperate and determined to fix? That he felt he needed a miracle to do so? And how did I not see any of it? What was he looking for, and why couldn't he just talk to me?

When I get back to the office the lights are off and everyone's gone. Evelyn's desk has been cleared of her photos, and postcards, and little knickknacks, and I realize I never said goodbye.

There's a note on Feldman's door saying he's closed early to do some damage control about the Morris debacle. He reminds me that we have a DistaGrieve service in the morning, and that he'll be operating one of the cameras to insure it goes smoothly and one more thing doesn't get "cocked up." How lovely. What lovely language. When I remove the note, the door opens a crack and I see the light from Nemo's tank is on. So I go in, and sit at Feldman's desk, and watch him swim for a while.

I never had to take the Fish Test.

Before all of this, before Gene died, and Ravanel, and the money problems, Feldman was one of our customers. He'd usually come in alone, sit in the back corner of the restaurant, and read the paper—the obituaries of course—while he ate. Afterwards I'd bring him his check, and then he'd ask for a to-go box, and then I would explain the nature of a buffet.

Then one night Feldman came by just after I'd locked up. I was still reeling from the Ravanel news. Burton had been arrested that afternoon. The restaurant was technically shutdown, and I wasn't supposed to have any customers, but I was too tired to care. I let him in. Feldman helped himself to what was left of the buffet, but instead of going to his usual table, he sat with me. He asked what was wrong.

"What makes you think something is wrong?" I said.

"Have you seen your face?" he said.

So while Feldman ate, I told him everything.

At first he didn't say anything. He just sat there, playing with the remnants of his beef and broccoli. "Huh," he finally said. "What is it that they say? 'What doesn't kill us makes us stronger?'"

"I think that's bullshit. It's a lie we tell ourselves to feel better."

"Yeah," he said. "Probably. But still, bad things happen, and though they may not make you stronger, if you're smart, they can make you money."

Then Feldman asked if I cried at Gene's funeral.

"Of course," I said.

"And now? Knowing everything you that you do, everything that he did, could you cry for him now?"

I thought about it. I admitted that though I had cried for Gene since I learned what he'd done, it had been different. I wasn't grief exactly, but something else.

Then Feldman smiled and asked if I was looking for work.

Our DistaGrieve service is Feldman's latest innovation. For an extra ninety-five dollars we'll record the ceremony, and then burn the footage to a DVD for family members that want to attend, but don't have the time or the money.

But today that seems to mean everyone. The entire family. Feldman and I are the only ones here. There's the deceased of course, and Father Bryan from St. Luke's, but he doesn't count. He's essentially a professional just like us.

Feldman hands me a video camera. "Keep your shots tight," he says. "Zoom in a lot. Let's not advertise the fact that there's not too many people here."

"There's no one here," I say, but Feldman waves this off. He tells me to get some footage of the tombstone.

So I get some footage of the tombstone.

It reads: *Gone but not forgotten.*

I get some more shots of questionable usefulness: the leaden sky, the treetops swaying in the breeze, two squirrels fighting over an empty Doritos bag.

Then Feldman says it's time to begin the service. He positions one camera on a tripod in front of Father Bryan and the casket. The other he handholds a few feet from me.

"Okay," he whispers, "go ahead. Mourn."

I go through my routine. I think about how it felt to lose something only to learn none of it was real. I think about the times I catch Connie staring at me, and the way she smiles, and how I know it's love but feels more like pity. I think about the future.

But it doesn't work. Nothing happens. I scrunch my eyes tight, try to squeeze the tears out, but nothing comes.

"What's the problem?" Feldman says.

I shake my head.

"What is that? What does that mean?"

"I don't know," I say. "I can't do it. I can't cry."

"Jesus Christ," Feldman yells.

Father Bryan clears his throat, checks his watch.

"I don't need this right now," Feldman says. "Just try harder. You can do it. You're better than this."

But I'm not sure I am.

"Why didn't I ever have to take the Fish Test?" I say.

"What?"

"I'm the only one, right? So why me? Why didn't I have to take it?"

"I don't know. You didn't need it."

"What? What does that mean?"

Feldman sighs, and stares at the ground, scanning it from left to right as if the answer is etched into the dirt and he is unable to find it. The camera, though still pointed at me, begins to droop in his hands. "Do you remember the night I offered you a job?" he says. "I asked if you had cried for your husband after everything that had happened?"

"Yes. So?"

"And you told me that you had. In spite of what he did, in spite of what you thought you knew about him, about your marriage, you still cried. Don't you get it? You've been crying for strangers since the beginning."

He's right. He's right, and the truth of it hits me like something physical, something real. Like something I haven't felt in a long time. And even though it's the saddest, most pathetic-sounding thing I've ever heard, and even though the cameras are rolling, and Feldman and Father Bryan are staring at me, I can't help but laugh.

And laugh.

And laugh.

Safety

by Lydia Fitzpatrick

In the gym, the children are stretching in rows. Their arms are over their heads, their right elbows cupped in left palms. Class is almost over, and this is the wind-down—that is what the gym teacher calls it—though the children move constantly, flexing their toes inside their sneakers, shifting their feet, canting their hips, biting their lips, because they are young, and their bodies are still new to them, a constant experiment. The gym teacher counts softly, one, two, three, four, and before five there is a sound that reminds a boy in the back row of the sound a bat makes when it hits a baseball perfectly. In the front row, a girl thinks it is the sound of lightning, not lightning in real life, because it is sunny out and because she can't remember ever hearing real lightning, but like lightning on TV, when the storm comes all at once. Next to her, her best friend thinks it is a sound like when her mother drives her into the city and the car first enters the tunnel, only this sound is sharper than that one and stays within its lines, and she is not inside it. One boy recognizes the sound. He has been to the range with his father and brother, and he has worn headphones and stood a safe distance and watched the sound jerk his father's arm and push his brother off balance. This boy is the first to let his elbow drop.

The gym teacher is thinking *five*, and then he knows. He looks to the door that leads to outside, to the ESL trailers, to the walkway that connects the elementary school to its middle school, because that is where the shot has come from, and there is a throb of hope for the girl who teaches ESL, who has just moved here and still bakes brownies for the teachers' lounge. The gym teacher is calm, and in his wind-down voice he tells the children to be quiet, completely quiet, and to run into the boys' locker room. The gym teacher is old, has been at this school for decades, and with each passing year, the children like him more and listen to him less, but they know to be afraid from the carefulness in his voice—they are not talked to carefully, except when they ask questions about death and divorce—and at first their fear is only for the tone of his voice, but then they remember the sound. They run, and their sneakers are the sort that light up with each footfall and their shoelaces whip against polished wood, and the gym teacher is not worried they will trip, but that they will stop—because they are the age when rules are God and shoelaces must be tied—but they don't stop, and they don't trip. There are eighteen of them. They are as fast and graceful as he has ever seen them.

When they reach the locker room, one boy grabs the gym teacher's sleeve. It is September, and he has not yet memorized their names, but he knows the boy's brother was a student of his years ago and the boy's father is back from the war. The boy whispers, "Gun." He is the one who recognized the sound and he has worried, as he sprinted across the basketball court, that the gym teacher might not know. The gym teacher nods, puts a finger to his lips. He is thinking means of egress. He is thinking police, hide, gun. He is thinking of his cell phone, which was a present from his son last Christmas, a tongue-in-cheek present, a comment on character, and it is in the pocket of his windbreaker on the back of the ladder chair in his kitchen at home.

The children have gathered around him when usually they scatter, and he can see in their eyes that they want to be picked up and held. One girl has forgotten the sound. She smiles and raises her hand. She has a question. She wants to know whether they should change out of their uniforms, but before she can ask, the gym teacher points to his office, which is in the middle of the locker room, and he tells them to lie on the floor behind his desk and to be quiet, and the carefulness drops from his voice—he can't help it, there are more shots, inside the school now, in the corridor, and a yell cut short.

As the children run, the gym teacher turns out the lights in the locker room and looks out into the lighted gym. The floor is perfectly bare, perfectly clean, glowing like the surface of a planet seen from afar. The cones and Frisbees and hula-hoops are back in their bins, and there is nothing to show that a class meets this period. Through the windows of the double doors he sees pale yellow wall tiles (they are the color of butter, of winter sun, but the tiles are more a constant in his world than butter or pale suns, and so when he sees those things he thinks they are the color of the school). The boy whose father is just back from the war, the one who recognized the sound, watches the gym teacher look to the doors, and he wishes the gym teacher were his father, because the gym teacher is old and afraid, and his father has only been afraid twice and both times were at the war, never at home, because here, he says, is paradise compared to there. This boy is the last into the office, and as he lies down next to the girl who thought of lightning, he goes on wishing for his father in the fervent way that children wish for things because they think those things are only an inch from their fingertips, almost in their grasp.

On the teacher's desk is the blue parachute the children play with on Fridays. On Fridays, they grip the silk and make it ripple and buck, they run underneath it and around it, but one of its seams is split, and the gym teacher meant to take it home to his wife who would stitch it up as she has dozens of times before. Behind his desk, the children are lying in two neat rows, and he has seen children lie this way before, on the news, in other countries, but not these children, his children, and he almost tells them to get up, that it is tempting fate to lie this way, but there are more shots, closer, in the cul-de-sac of classrooms across from the gym, and the gym teacher grabs the parachute and spreads it over them, and they are so small that it covers all eighteen of them easily, and at the thought of them—of how many and how small—his chest seizes, and he thinks that he will be the one to make a noise, but then he hears the clang of the gym doors opening and the long sigh of them swinging shut and his fear becomes the biggest thing he's ever felt. It is so much bigger than him that for a second it eclipses him entirely.

The gym teacher cannot think, and then, just as suddenly, he can. He turns out the lights in his office and the parachute is not quite as dark as the shadows around it—the silk has a gleam—but it is the best he can do. He crouches under his desk. He is between the children and the door, and he whispers to them one more time, "Do not make a sound. Do not move." Under the parachute, a girl pees without thinking of holding it. She feels it hot and soaking the seat of her gym shorts, and the parachute is light on her face. On Fridays this is the best feeling, and she thinks of that, of how she is getting to feel it today even though it is not a Friday. There are footsteps moving across the gym. A boy thinks, Dad. A girl thinks, Mom, Mom, Mom. One boy thinks it is the principal, because the principal is the only one who walks through the halls when they're empty. One girl begins to count silently. She panics sometimes—when she sees the road disappearing too fast under the car's tires; when the train cuts through their town, its whistle blaring; when she is in the swing at the park and finds herself too high—and her parents tell her to count, to breathe, to count and breathe, and they count with her, lead her from one number to the next.

The footsteps are slow. The gym teacher knows this means it is him, and it means something about him too. The gym teacher is curled around his knees. He has never made himself so small. Behind him, the parachute moves with each of their breaths.

There is a new noise. A clang of metal on metal. The boy who recognized the shot does not know what this sound is, and he realizes now there was comfort in knowing. He does not love Fridays and the parachute. He does not love anything that hems him in, and his mother tells him that even as a baby he did not like to be held. He edges out from under the parachute. He is between the wall and the girl who thought of lightning, and it is dark, but he can see the gym teacher's coat rack branching over him and he can see the windows that line the walls of the office and look out into the locker room. Deep in the dark there is a red haze from the exit sign over the door that leads to outside, to the ESL trailers, and to the walkway to the middle school where his brother is, and the boy could run that walkway in twenty-two seconds—he has timed himself on a watch that is both waterproof and a calculator—but his brother does not like him to come to the middle school. Instead, his brother meets the boy on the hill above the soccer field, where there is a tree that has a disease that has made its bark peel and a path that leads through the woods to their house.

The clanging noise shakes in the air and gives way to the footsteps. The girl counts thirty, thirty-one. He is close, the gym teacher thinks, by the showers, whose dripping is the metronome of his days. The showers are separated from the office by three banks of lockers, and as he thinks of the lockers, he realizes that was the clanging sound, metal on metal—the butt of the gun or the muzzle. The children's things are inside the lockers and strewn around them, their backpacks and jackets and lunch bags and dioramas—they are that age, when teachers tell them to pick their favorite place in the world and fit it in a shoebox and they can—and the man with the gun will see these things, and he will know they are here. The gym teacher shifts into a squat and one of his ankles cracks. He doesn't know what he'll do when the door opens, but he keeps his eye on the dark square of the window next to the door. The footsteps are closer and closer and closer and far away there are screams, and a girl—the youngest in the class—has heard these screams before, at the hospital, when she was having an arm set and down the hall someone else was having something worse. Next to her, a boy wishes for something to hold onto. His palms burn with the need, and he finds the girl's hand next to his and grabs it, and she thinks this is like the hospital too, where everyone was holding hands.

He is here. There is a change in the darkness in the window that the gym teacher feels more than sees (just as he feels his wife's absence some nights, when she is sleepless and moves through the house below him), and then the change is clearer: he can see the man's glasses catch the red light of the exit sign. He can see the nose of the gun moving toward the window. There is a clink, a knife on a plate. Fifty-six, the girl counts, and the gym teacher knows the glass will splinter, he knows how this ends, but behind him the boy crouched under the coat rack sees something different: a half-foot down the gun's barrel, where the shoulder strap attaches, there is a dangling medal, a slim silver oval barely bigger than a thumbnail, but big enough for the boy to recognize it. It is a saint medal, the saint whose job it is to protect soldiers, and the boy knows the saint's name because it is the same as his own, and he knows the medal because his mother gave it to his father years ago, before you were born, she tells him, before your brother was born, when your father left for the first time.

The gun drops from the window, and the boy does not hesitate. He is up. He opens the door and slips through it, his body filled with the certainty of it, with a wish fulfilled, his father, and as he turns the gun is ready for him. It is inches from him. Dad, the boy thinks, even as he realizes that the man is not tall enough to be his father, is not tall enough to be a father at all. In life, the boy has been fearless—he trusts the dark, trusts the slimmest branch, trusts that he alone can fly—but he looks at the gun and his mind goes cold and cavernous.

"Where's your class?" the man says, his voice muffled by a ski mask.

The boy hesitates for a moment—he does not think of protecting his class, of protecting the girl who is his favorite, who is under the parachute, trying to remember the prayer that her grandmother mumbles in Polish each night—for a moment he hesitates because he cannot speak. Then that moment is over, and he is still alive, and he says, "Outside."

"Outside," they gym teacher hears, and he thinks that this might save them, but the silence grows long and he does not know what it means. He is listening for sirens, wishing for sirens in the fervent way that children wish, as though his chest is opening to dispatch some part of him that will find the sirens and usher them here. Behind him, the children know that for the first time they are hiding without wanting to be found.

The boy raises his eyes and looks up the long line of the gun to the medal. It *is* his father's gun. The boy can see it here, and he can see it locked in the case in the hall between the door to his room and the door to his brother's room, where it glows in the way things precious and forbidden glow—the grandfather clock with the damp brass gears and the ostrich egg with foreign letters inked on its curves and the tiny crystal bottle on his mother's dresser—and the constellation of these things is as sacred and eternal as anything up in the sky, and the boy cannot believe the gun is here and its case is empty.

"Let's go," the man says, and his voice is muffled, but there is something strained in it that the boy recognizes. The boy looks up, past the medal, to the mask, which is a ski hat with holes cut for the mouth and nose and eyes, and over the eye holes are glasses that could be anyone's, except that they are his brother's. They are across the table from him every morning, slanted towards a book whose pages are dusted with the crumbs of the toast his mother makes. They were across the table from him this morning.

The boy reaches out and puts a finger to the nose of the gun, and it is warm. He has never touched the gun before, and his brother yanks it away, and the medal jingles, this tiny silver noise, and his brother grabs his hand.

Under the desk, the gym teacher listens to them walk away and he begins to cry. He has always thought that you could *know*, that right and wrong were like bones beneath the skin—hidden but there, waiting to be laid bare—and his hands are empty and he cannot weigh the one against the seventeen. The girl who is counting hits a hundred and starts over again at one, and the boy's brother pulls him towards the emergency exit, and the boy has dreamed of this, in certain stretches of homeroom, when he is filling a sheet with cursive L's, he has dreamed of his brother taking him out of class and letting him sit on the back of his bike as they coast down the hill into the town to the store with the miniature models of helicopters and tanks and dragons that are all the color of flour, waiting to be painted with brushes whose bristles are thin as eyelashes, but even as he dreams this, he knows it will not happen because his brother prefers to be alone, likes to have space, though his mother says that as a baby his brother was the one that liked to be held.

They are at the door, and his brother pushes it open with a hip so that he can keep one hand on the gun. The gym teacher watches a wedge of light stretch across the locker room, the benches, the bookbags, and he is waiting for a child to speak, to cough—it is that season, when their noses run and their lips chap—but they are silent, and the light recedes, and he tells the children to stay quiet and that he will be back.

Outside, the air is cool and sweet. The light is too bright—it makes the boy think of Sundays, when their mother takes them to the movies, and the boy loves the movies, cannot sit close enough to the screen, and when the movie is over and they step out of the theater, the fact of the world outside is a shock to him, an insult. The boy's brother lets go of his hand, and the bell rings, blaring from loud-speakers in the corridors and classrooms, from speakers mounted on the corners of the ESL trailer. It is time for lunch, but no one comes out of the trailer, and the school is still. There is the soccer field. The grass arches away from the wind, and they cross the parking lot to the field, and the boy looks back over his shoulder and sees a girl lying on the sidewalk next to the ESL trailer. She has fallen with one ear against the pavement, and the boy recognizes the girl. She is two grades above him, with dark hair and a red birthmark on her cheek in the shape of a cloud. Her face has gone so pale that even the birthmark is drained of color, and be-yond her, on the steps of the trailer, is another woman and from the way she is lying the boy can tell that her face will look the same.

Under the parachute, the girl who thought of lightning is thinking of her grandfather, who is the only person she knows to have died—his heart had been good but turned bad—and her own chest hurts, and she wonders if it is her heart turning inside her. A boy begins to shake. His teeth are chattering and he puts a finger between them so they do not make a sound, and he has never thought of himself as truly separate from his mother, and yet he is sure that at her desk in the office in the city she does not know what is happening to him and cannot feel his fear. In the years to come, he will think of this over and over, of how she did not know.

The boy's brother is breathing fast behind the mask, and the boy knows that he shot the girl and the woman. The tip of the gun was warm, but the boy cannot make sense of it or of why he is following his brother, crossing the field at the same angle he does every afternoon. From the door to the locker room, the gym teacher watches the two boys—they are both boys, he can see that now—as they walk up the hill towards the woods. There is a dead girl on the pavement and on the steps of the trailer a woman moans, and when the boys are far enough away the gym teacher runs to the woman. It is the ESL teacher, and he puts his fingers to her neck and says, please, please, please. Eighty-eight, the girl counts, her lips careful with the numbers, eighty-nine. The parachute is so hot. The silk begins to stick to them, to foreheads and noses and knees.

At the top of the hill, where there is the tree with the peeling bark and where the path to the boy's home begins, there is a cross stuck in the ground. It is two pieces of a yardstick that the boy recognizes because his mother used it to stir a can of paint—one end is the blue of their kitchen—and now it has been broken in two and nailed together. The boy's brother stops at the cross and says, "They'll ask you why." Every word comes out like a splinter, like he is in pain, and the boy says, "Are you crying?"

The gym teacher hears sirens, faint as wind chimes, as he puts his mouth to the woman's and exhales.

"Listen to me," the boy's brother says, and he gets down on his knees. "They're going to ask you why."

His brother's glasses are fogged. The ski cap is his mother's. It is the one she wears when she shovels snow and it smells of a dog, though they've never had one, and he does not know how to square these ordinary things with the way his brother is shaking—not gently, but wildly—as he pulls the gun over his shoulder and points it at him.

"Are you going to shoot me?" the boy says.

The girl counts one hundred and stops, because her fear has dissolved, is a memory now. The gym teacher puts his fingers to the woman's neck again, and this time there is nothing. Another girl hears the sirens and thinks of her dog and the way he howls with his throat arched whenever he hears a siren and of how he will be howling now, in her house, which is nearby, pacing the halls and filling the empty rooms with that sound.

The boy begins to cry. Not because he is afraid of being shot—he cannot think what that might feel like, though he has seen it in games and on TV, though he has seen the holes burned through the paper targets at the range—but because he is afraid that his brother hates him, has always hated him. That must have been why, one time, his brother had hit him in the mouth hard enough to swell his lip.

The gym teacher looks up the hill and he sees that the boys are the same height—the boy with the gun is kneeling—and he sees where the gun is pointed, and he gets up and begins to run across the soccer field. The seventeen are safe, under the parachute, but already he knows that it won't matter against this one, that that is not how the scales work.

"I'm not going to shoot you," the boy's brother says, "because I'm not crazy. You tell them that. That I'm not crazy."

The boy nods, but he will not tell anyone what his brother said, not his mother, not his father, not ever. He will insist that his brother was silent, that his brother was crazy, and he will dream of the girl with the cloud-shaped birthmark. With the gun, the boy's brother motions for him to turn towards the tree with the peeling bark, and the boy turns. He is facing the path that leads home and he has timed himself on this path, too. In two minutes and seven seconds he can be home, where his mother is pulling clothes from the drier. She straightens, hearing the sirens, and it takes her a moment to unravel the sound, to register how many and how close, and she thinks there must be a fire—it has been a dry summer, a dry fall—and she goes to the window and looks towards the school. The boy can't tell if the sirens are getting closer. They seem to be carried on the wind, like they are coming from the trees, and even though he knows this isn't so, he looks up at the leaves that are red and brown and thrashing.

The gym teacher is halfway across the soccer field, and in two months, when the school reopens, his wife will walk from goal to goal for hours, eyes on the grass, looking for the gleam of a bullet in the dirt. Under the parachute, the children think of lightning and tunnels. They think of the gym teacher who said he'd come back and of mothers and fathers and of the sound of the man's voice when he said, "Let's go," and how you are never supposed to go. Later, when the policeman finds them, when he pulls up the parachute, and tells them they are safe, he will not be able to forget it: how still the children were, how silent, how they didn't move a muscle.

The boy looks from the trees to the school. The gym teacher is running across the field, and he is old and slow, and from this high on the hill it seems like he is barely moving. The gym teacher's heart is battering at his lungs, his chest is burning, and the boy only watches him for a second, but it is too long—his brother turns towards the field. The sirens are everywhere now. His brother is breathing in the way that means you're hurt. The gym teacher is across the field, and he is afraid, but with his next breath his fear goes, and he does not know why, because the gun is aimed at him now, but he thinks of a morning years ago, when his son got a shoelace caught in the mower, and the gym teacher cut the lace with a pocket knife and watched the panic roll out of his son's eyes, and an hour later, in the hospital, he will die, whispering to his wife about a knife through cotton.

The boy hears the shot and wishes he did not understand the sound. He begins to run, and the leaves slide under his sneakers and he keeps his eyes on the path because there is a root up ahead that tripped him once, walking home, and his knee had bled, and his brother had looked at him and kissed his knee and said, "What's the point in crying?" The boy leaps over the root. He is running fast enough that the trees blur around him, and the gym teacher feels the hot rip of the bullet, and up on the hill there is another shot.

The Emigrants
by Colette Langlois

31.03.2070 station 1 / If you come, bring bamboo.

Last night I slipped under the cover with James, and though he didn't say anything—hadn't been able to speak for days—a slight pressure when our arms touched answered he felt me there and was glad.

Then I thought of the bamboo sheets I once owned, their soft weight both warm and cool, their spring fern colour and faint wooden scent. I can't remember whether they ended up at the Salvation Army thrift store or in one of the boxes that went to the salvage area at the dump with all the other too-heavy luxuries we couldn't take with us. We who made this one-way journey stopped talking about things like that when we realized it was a kind of torture for each other, and those kinds of memories were best kept to ourselves.

James is dead. Sometime in the night two of us were breathing, then only one. That faint contact of skin when my arm nudged his as I lay down was the most we ever touched. I can only hope my presence in those last hours brought him some comfort.

Later I'll put him outside with the others, but for now he's lying where I left him, under the weightless silver sheet. Even after thirty years I still hate those flimsy covers, reminders of long ago over-baked potatoes. I refuse to call them blankets, whatever their little yellow labels might say. The product of some mind that thought the only purpose of blankets was to keep us warm.

*

The responsibility of reporting now rests with me. The complicated processes we once used to choose a successor each time a lead rapporteur died—usually culminating in acclamations, rarely a secret ballot required—all seem so quaint now. Our concern for fairness, avoiding unnecessary conflict and hurt feelings. How important those things seemed when there were more of us. By the time we were down to four we settled it with a crib tournament. James and I went with rock-paper-scissors.

No contest this time.

I'm writing in the garden, the only place I can stand to be now. The fibre-optic strands funnel in the scant sunlight, and the plants give off a slight humidity that makes breathing just a bit easier. They grow surprisingly well here, as I expect James documented in much more technical detail. Aside from the cold, the red planet is naturally kind to them, with plenty of subsurface water and minerals in the dust that, mixed with our compost, provide all the nourishment they need. About the garden: I should tell you a few things, in case James forgot to mention them, in case you come and no one's left. For example, it is important to blow on the carrot tops. In the still air they droop, weakened, until they touch the ground and turn yellow. But a little breath, like the breezes from home, seems to give them the strength to grow sturdy and green.

I will do my best to remember anything else that you might not think of on your own and leave notes for you. Just in case.

I'm dreading moving James's body. For one thing, it means putting on my space suit. Also awkward and silver, like the sheets. It has always annoyed me that everything in space is silver. As though all the imagination got used up on the mechanics of things, with nothing left over for colours and textures.

He's light enough after being sick all these months that I could probably carry him, but I'll use a cart anyway. It wouldn't do to throw my back out, being alone.

I'll need to be much more careful from now on.

*

I'm in the garden again, and it's done. James is outside with the others. The botanist has joined the two medical doctors and gaggle of engineers frozen naked and staring empty-eyed up into eternity.

And then there was only the psychologist.

The most useless and unskilled of the entire group, but someone at Headquarters must have thought it would be a good idea to include one. Five hundred years ago they would have sent a Jesuit along on an expedition like this, but in 2042 they wanted a PsyD. And now here I am. Who would have bet on this old girl to be the last?

About the arrangement of the bodies: Headquarters told us to preserve them for future study, but they didn't give specifics. I wonder what those hypothetical researchers to come will make of our artistry. Maybe they'll think we invented some new religion, when the truth is it was only a mix of aesthetic pleasure-seeking and boredom. We started out lining them up, but later someone—I think Sonny, the water engineer—had the idea we should arrange them in a circle, with toes touching. Back then the circle was only a little more than half formed. Now there's just one wedge left, for me, although I don't know how I'll get to it in the end.

I took my time getting ready to move James. The death-smells of emptied bowels and decomposing tissue, I'll be honest, made me retch, but I lingered anyway, knowing these would likely be the last human odours I would ever breathe, apart from my own. Outside, I jumped on his knees to break them so his legs would go straight like the others', and when they cracked under my feet I nearly threw up in my helmet. I should have positioned him when I first woke, when he was still a little warm and the rigour had not yet set in, instead of wasting time writing and crying in the garden. I would say I'll know better for next time, but there won't be a next time, will there?

*

It's occurred to me I may seem a little flippant about James's death, and I apologize if anyone's left who cared for him and is offended, as unlikely as that is. After all, those of us who came on this one-way trip were chosen partly for our lack of human ties to the blue-green planet. Enticed here by advertisements hinting at adventure and new beginnings, perhaps not unlike those that lured my third great-grandparents from England to their Saskatchewan homestead two centuries ago.

Though James and I were alone for over a year, I still feel I hardly knew him, and for that I'm sorry. He was a soft-spoken man. He had a wife and child once, I think, killed in a car accident on a Florida holiday in the 20s. He liked spinach and backgammon. I will miss him.

*

About the bamboo: I don't expect you to bring all the machinery and materials to make sheets or even to know where to begin with that whole process. We'll find other uses, food to start, though I admit I like the idea that one day, even after I'm gone, bamboo sheets will exist on the red planet. I can't say what insights and lucky coincidences and inventions will be required between now and then. I just have faith the mere imagining that something's possible can be enough to set it on the trajectory to being. Like Da Vinci's helicopter sketches. They waited four and a half centuries on paper, but the day came when they flew.

Anyone reading this should be aware there won't be many more messages, maybe none. The solar cells that power the transmitter are failing. James noticed and warned me about this a few months back. At least the water and air systems are holding, even though all the parts were supposed to have been replaced years ago by later missions. The ones that never came, let me remind you.

"Delayed" was the official word. "Budget cuts" the truth, revealed in one final unsigned message, right before Headquarters shut everything down. After some discussion, we agreed to keep that last transmission a secret to avoid getting anyone else in trouble. However, after revisiting the issue with the surviving red planet settlers, i.e., myself, I've decided after all this time to spill it.

Whichever board or committee made the decision to cut us off knew it was our death sentence. Of course, they also knew they could get away with it. Who would have bothered to organize protests and petitions? Who would have cared, given our lack of human ties to the blue-green planet?

All I want is some shred of accountability. I don't expect you to do anything about it now, but it makes me feel better to know you know I know. If you're even reading this.

That's all for now. The carrots need my breath. / cmb
<u>Send</u>

*

Red Jacket, Assiniboia East. September 8, 1885
Dear Sister,

I regret I have not been able to write to you since my last letter from Montreal. We have had much to do to secure provisions and make a cabin livable for winter, which our neighbours who arrived two years ago tell me is fierce and long in this part of the country. The journey was as the agent forewarned: the prairies seem endless, days and days to cross by train, and, I'm told, they continue days more to the west of us all the way to the Rocky Mountains. For now, we live under a warm sun and cloudless blue sky, with green and golden fields all around save a stand of trees they call cottonwood along the small creek that runs nearby. Your nephews are growing strong with hard work, fresh air, and sunshine, and your nieces lovelier by the day as every breath fills their lungs with Nature's raw beauty.

Lucille is finding the conditions harsh, I fear, and suffering for the lack of female company. I assure you the cabin is no poorer than some of the lodgings you and I knew in our childhood, but it must be remembered my wife was raised with more comforts than you and me, and it is to be expected she would find this change in her circumstances difficult. I thought she was bearing it admirably until the last of our trunks arrived and we discovered the one containing all the quilts, so carefully stitched over countless evenings, had gone missing. I do believe her heart broke at that moment. In a poor effort to raise her spirits, I joked I would ride off every dawn to hunt buffalo and wolves until I gathered enough pelts for us all to have as fine sleeping robes as any Sioux chief, but I fear this only caused her more distress. I am sorry necessity required me to trade Mother's little pewter pin box, among other small treasures, for a few of the Hudson's Bay Company blankets. I do hope you will forgive me this loss. Our new blankets are plain, but made from heavy wool that will keep us warm in our beds through the winter.

I must end here, Dear Sister. The trader who has kindly agreed to deliver this letter to Moosomin Station will soon depart. I trust you and Jimmy and my little nieces are well and wish you good health until I may write again.

Your devoted brother,

J.M.B.

*

08.04.2070 station 1 / I saw what you did.

I'm not even sure where to start this report now. From the beginning, I guess.

The latest dust storm ended overnight, and today I was able to get out to complete all the routine checks and maintenance. The winds were especially fierce, and the cleanup took much more time than usual. First, I climbed the outside of the dome over the garden to sweep off the solar panels. The station's layout from that perspective reminds me of a medieval cathedral, one that endured extensive additions and renovations every hundred and fifty years. A few saints and gargoyles would fit nicely. My dusting job worked: the lights have stopped flickering now.

Next I went down to the main roof to inspect for the beginnings of fractures or other damage. Nothing to report. The robots who assembled the station before our arrival clearly took pride in their craftsmanship. They've all long since been pillaged for their parts, donating their vital organs to keep water pumps and climate control systems operating. To keep us humans alive. I know they weren't sentient (I haven't gone crazy, if that's what you were thinking), but it seems unfair to me how they ended up despite all their diligence and industriousness.

After the roof, I walked the building perimeter. No damage to the walls either. They are smooth and the same silver as my suit, designed to be easily visible from approaching vessels—the ones you never sent. They glow reddish orange in the faint sunlight.

Last, I visited each of the solar panels arrayed around the station. Again, no damage, just in need of cleaning. All the storage cells are in good shape, except for those connected to the transmitter. Very little charge left—this may well be the last time you hear from me. If anyone's left to hear. After what you did.

By the time I finished my spit and polishing, sunset was near and both moons had risen. I checked on my fellow settlers, also dusty, but otherwise as I last left them. The summer breezes will blow them clean again.

Eight women and eleven men, a mandala for the stars to gaze down upon. The oldest ones, from twenty years ago, are desiccated but otherwise intact. They will start to thaw in a few weeks, but in these anaerobic conditions they don't decompose, and most nights they will refreeze anyway. No wild animals to feast on them and scatter their bones. No worms to eat them from the inside out. They will be here like this until our swollen red sun swallows the solar system, then explodes everything into stardust to start it all over.

I have a childhood memory of a brief stop on a long road trip at a graveyard somewhere between the Qu'Appelle and Assiniboine rivers, near the Manitoba border. Weathered tombstones, some sinking into the soggy ground, others toppled over on their faces and lying under two inches of water. Wind snaking through the flooded grasses and shaking the tops of the cottonwoods. Somewhere beneath the watery surface, the blind, muddy bones of ancestors born on the other side of the Atlantic, who once must have found solace standing or kneeling in that quiet patch of earth on the outskirts of their village. As we who came here found solace in our mandala.

I still had nearly an hour of oxygen left. I lay down in my wedge as I sometimes do and nudged my frozen neighbours in greeting. The twenty of us all together again. The mandala complete. Jupiter rising between the two moons, and the shimmer of the terrifyingly near asteroid belt between us and our giant neighbour.

Spring is here and the days are lengthening. About -10 degrees now, quite bearable compared to the typical -103 winter's day. If only I could take my suit off.

Spring. Olfactory memory is the strongest and the most easily recovered. I conjured up the smells of late April on the blue-green planet. Fresh grass in wet peat. Melting dog shit. Half-decomposed leaves. Thirty years, with no idea what spring smells like here. If I ever do find out it will be with my last breath. Death by hypercapnia, which I imagine to be quick and painless although I don't know for sure, since none of us went that way.

They screened us for suicidal tendencies, of course. Even now, despite what you did, I have no intention of hastening the end of my life. I am far too curious about the possible endings to this strange story of mine, and all the moments in between.

But if there were a way to arrange it, if I could be sure I was about to die from say, a massive heart attack within the next 120 seconds, and if I could only have the time to strip naked, then hold my breath long enough to run out the door, lie down, and get into position with the others, I would. From my place in the circle I would open my eyes wide and inhale through my nostrils, sacrificing the few seconds I might have had remaining just to grasp that one last bit of knowledge.

The blue-green planet twinkled a few degrees above the horizon, becoming brighter and more distinct as the sun sank and disappeared. I lifted my hand and waved with my clumsy silver arm. On the way here, if you can believe my naiveté, I imagined a crop of fashion designers inspired by our expedition—for a brief time before our departure we were minor celebrities—creating new and improved space suits in a variety of colours and cuts to flatter various body types to be sent along with the next vessel and with each vessel to follow. New trends for every season. Well, it was a pleasant thought for a while.

As I lay in the mandala, imagining the scent of the red planet spring and sleek fuchsia space suits, Earth suddenly shone bigger and brighter than I had ever seen it before. An illusion created by the dust still floating in the meagre atmosphere, I thought, but alluring nonetheless, like a candle in a distant window on a black, pre-electricity night. Then there was a moment when awe and wonder at the loveliness of it switched to horror as I realized what you must have done for that to happen, right before the starburst flash, brief fireball, and complete darkness.

*

Twenty-three years since I last had news of you, I have no idea what unsolvable political crisis or technological fuck-up could have made blowing up the entire planet inevitable, but I have to tell you, from here it all seems pretty unnecessary. I guess I'm in shock.

I wonder if the moon is still there, and what will happen to it now. Catapulted into the sun, flung into outer space, or left to inherit the blue-green planet's orbit and continue its silent path in peace?

I am going to send this. I waited. I considered. Here it is: even if there is only the most infinitesimal chance someone is still left to read this, sending these words is the right thing to do. Whether or not anyone receives them is not my concern.

I wish someone would breathe on me the way I breathe on the carrots. / cmb <u>Send</u>

*

Red Jacket, Assiniboia East. 12 April 1889
Dear Sister,

My news is sorrowful, and I pray you do not find your-self alone as you read it. Yesterday we buried Lucille. Her heart failed her, the doctor said, though he had no need to tell me. To think she would have had her fiftieth birthday this September. Though I often feared for her when she was bearing our children, always mindful of how you and I lost our own dear Mother, once our last was born I imagined she was safe and we would grow old together. How foolish I was.

Poor little Leo is inconsolable. Being the youngest, he was still accustomed to clinging to his mother's skirts and climbing into her lap, an indulgence for which, I now re-gret, I often reproached her. Amelia and James have taken him and Sarah into their home, where they will stay until after the harvest or perhaps longer. It gives me some com-fort that, though deprived of their Ma, the littlest ones will know at least the care of their gentle sister. The others will remain with me to help ready the fields and sow the crops, which must be accomplished soon, the land and elements caring nought for our grief.

She is laid to rest in the yard of our new little brick church, I assure you, as good a Christian burial as she might have had in England. My neighbour the Swede built her a coffin from lumber that I believe he had intended to use to repair his barn, and would accept no payment in re-turn. His wife brought us breads and stews made in the style of their country, and was most kind to the children. It grieves me Lucy never sought to befriend her, nor the Ger-man ladies who live nearby and who, when they learned of her passing, also came to clean the house and attend to us. Though their English is halting and they do not share our faith, they are of good heart and would have made her fine companions. All of our fellow countrymen regrettably dwell at some distance from our little homestead.

The coffin was plain but well made. It only pained me to think of sweet Lucy lying on its bare wood, and, as there was no finer fabric to be had for a lining, God forgive me, I placed inside one of the Company blankets she so detested. Aside from you, Dear Sister, only Amelia knows, and like me she thought it was the best to be done for her mother under the circumstances.

I am told the Reverend spoke well at the service, though I confess my head was so filled with other thoughts I hardly heard him or recall what he said. The little church was full of our friends, and even our Catholic and Lutheran neighbours came to pay their respects. Two young North-West Mounted Police officers who boarded with us for a few days when they were caught in a terrible blizzard last winter, on hearing of our loss, rode up from White Bear Post. In their fine scarlet coats they made a handsome addition to the funeral procession. I am certain Lucy would have been pleased.

I fear in some of my letters to you I have written things that may have cast my dear wife in an unfavourable light. I beg you to put those out of your mind as the unkind thoughts of an impatient and obstinate husband. I have had no true cause to judge her so harshly for her unhappiness here. She was raised a merchant's daughter, with many comforts, and had just hope and expectation of living her days as a merchant's wife. She was so until the decision, which was my own, and taken with greatest insistence, to uproot us from our homeland. She bore me fourteen children and was a most devoted mother. Though, as you surely remember, we both grieved deeply the loss of brave Henry at the brink of his manhood, I daresay it was she who comforted me more than I her in that darkest of times, when I could not find rest for the dreams of my beloved son sinking to his death in the Pacific. It is I who am at fault, having brought the sorrows of these recent years that broke her dear heart upon her, and for this I must and shall beg forgiveness to the last of my days.

Dear Sister, I am sorry to write with such melancholy, but I trust you of all people will grant me your pardon, for like our dear Mother you are disposed to see the greatest and most good in all, and possessed of a patience and understanding your wretched brother could never hope to find within himself.

I enclose a letter Lucy wrote only a week ago to her friend Mrs. Anson, and ask that you would deliver it in person along with the tidings of her passing, as I fear the dear lady will be most grieved. Perhaps you would also be so kind as to call upon Lucy's brother Charles and his family. Though I will write to him myself, I would wish you to convey my respects with the kindness and sympathy only you could.

Your devoted brother,
J.M.B.

*

12.04.2070 station 1 / I've been practising.

I count to ten, take a deep breath, open the door, and run. So far I've only been able to get about two-thirds of the way to our wheel before I can't help myself and let the air out. I blame it on the suit. Awkward and clunky as it is, it slows me down. Naked, I think I could get there in time, but I need to be sure.

As if this whole plan weren't already complicated enough, I thought of yet another problem after my practice run this morning. Most of the surface is fine dust and quite soft, but there are pebbles and larger rocks, some of them with razor-like edges. The smaller ones are what I worry about, because they're harder to see and shift from place to place with the wind.

My conclusion: I don't think I can pull off complete nudity. I might need my boots. I picture myself almost making it, then puncturing the ball of my foot on a sharp stone, crying out—and you can imagine the rest. The researchers would find the mandala with its one empty wedge and nineteen peaceful bodies almost god-like in their serenity. Nearby would be the corpse of a naked old woman, awkwardly clutching her foot and her face contorted with some mixture of pain, surprise, and profound disappointment.

No, I don't want to be that woman. I still have some sense of dignity. So in my breath-holding practice I must factor in a few extra seconds to take off my boots and toss them away before I get into position.

I am well aware the odds are close to nil that I will have the just-right notice of my impending death that will allow me to even attempt carrying out this sequence. But if it happens, I intend to be ready.

After my practice, I repeated all the routine checks. I have been experimenting with changing the order of tasks to get through them more quickly and was pleased I set a record today: four minutes and fifty-three seconds less than the previous one. It's not an obsession with efficiency, only that at seventy-something years of age, I would like to conserve my energy where I can. In any case, no structural damage or systems malfunctions to report. I will say now, conclusively, the transmitter batteries are completely gone. I held out some hope they would recharge at least a little after my last message, but after several days they fail to show the faintest sign of life.

*

Why am I still writing? One could say I went ahead and sent my last message, even after what you did, out of shock, with my internal processing of what had just happened incomplete. But I'm beyond that stage now.

Perhaps a sense of duty. We were, after all, sent here at considerable expense with the expectation we would notice things and report them, making our contribution to the collective knowledge of humankind. They screened us for qualities like diligence and responsibility. No social loafers on this mission. Given the slightest possibility someone survived total destruction of the planet and, even more improbably, was still picking up the signal, simple duty demanded I send that message.

But now? Now I no longer even have the means to transmit, yet I continue to write. Could I really still be clinging to some fine thread of hope? If someone survived the explosion of the blue-green planet. And if that someone received my final transmission. And if that someone had a way to travel here. And if, when that someone arrived, I was still around to let them in the door or they had the wherewithal to figure out how to open it themselves. And if they found this room and the systems were still functioning, so my words were still on this screen. Then ... what?

I tug a little on that fine thread and it stubbornly refuses to break. Am I deceiving myself into improbable hope, not wanting to admit I am only clinging to a habit, some vestige of normalcy in the face of a really fucked-up situation? Could it be these words are just a pathetic attempt at sorting out my thoughts, at maintaining sanity with some reasonable measure of comfort? That in the end I write only for myself?

I have no answers to these questions.

*

I have been lying in my little wedge in the mandala. It may seem morbid to you that I spend so much time with corpses. I, too, might have thought so once. When I left the blue-green planet, in my country it was customary to dispatch the dead to morgues, funeral homes, crematoria, and to leave the handling of the remains to professionals. Perhaps an afternoon or two might be spent in the company of an open coffin with the loved one's embalmed shell inside. Cosmetics artfully applied to give a semblance of peaceful sleep. More often a closed casket, or not even a whole body, only a small urn of ground bones and ash.

It was not always so. Once, in the not-so-distant past, bodies were laid out on kitchen tables, where they were washed, groomed, dressed, cried over by family members. Homes were small, and all the daily activities of cooking, bathing, nursing infants, mending clothes, conversing must have gone on all around. The men of the family, or perhaps a kind neighbour, would have built the coffin from whatever lumber was available, and loved ones would have laid the body inside and nailed it shut. There might have been an undertaker to dig the grave and cover it over, but even that task was often left to the mourners.

I was forty-one when I boarded the ship that brought us here. My parents had died in a plane crash when I was still in grad school, I was ten years divorced, had no children, no siblings, and had lost touch with any remaining aunts, uncles, cousins. Lack of ties to the blue-green planet.

Headquarters deserves some credit. They did at least put substantial thought and effort into selecting the right combination of people. Not only complementary skill sets, but a balance of gender, personality traits, values, interests. For the most part they succeeded. We were a remarkably harmonious group. A real community. Of course there were some limits. Most importantly, they screened us for fertility—a test I passed with flying colours, thanks to a hysterectomy two years earlier. As cold and indifferent as Headquarters could be, even they understood the absolute horror it would be to allow a baby into this living experiment.

So you see, this is my family. When I lie in my little wedge I feel no horror or revulsion toward my dead companions. Rather, I take comfort in their presence, the feelings and memories that resurface, the smiles and tears they bring. I have tapped into that ease and understanding of life and death all my ancestors must have had until a mere century or so before I left our planet. Here, in my part of the mandala, I feel only a sense of belonging, of being in my rightful place. Of being home.

*

131

There is one more observation I need to record. When I was looking up today, toward the dusk horizon where the blue-green planet should have been, I saw something. A handful of faint twinkles. I noticed them yesterday evening too, but today they are slightly bigger and I am certain I did not imagine them. They are approaching. Perhaps some of the debris field, a few molten rocks that will collide with this ball of red dust and complete your destruction. Or, dare I hope, perhaps a handful of ships carrying survivors. And bamboo.

Either way, I will be ready. / cmb <u>Send</u>

*

Red Jacket, Assiniboia East. October 24, 1889
Dear Sister,

I received your letter some weeks ago, and regret I have not been able to reply sooner. The harvest demanded every ounce of my physical strength so that, hungry as I was, for weeks I often fell asleep mid-supper and had to be nudged awake by one of the boys to stumble off to bed with my belly only half-full. The wheat was plentiful this year and the prices fair. I am relieved the children will all have new sets of clothing, those of the youngest having become quite threadbare with use. It pains me my dear wife is not here to partake with us in this long-hoped-for bounty. She might at last have allowed herself a few small luxuries, and perhaps her hopes might have been rekindled and her spirits lifted by the sights of the full pantry and all her brood in tidy little trousers and dresses trundling off to the Sunday service.

Your words as always brought me great comfort. It eased my soul to read that Lucy, though with some trepidation, also approached our journey with a measure of excitement and anticipation, and not merely in obedience to her husband's stubborn will. I am grateful she so confided in you, and that you have seen fit to now share those confidences with me.

You asked, most delicately, if I might in the next year or two remarry. I think not. Lucy's memory is yet too dear, and I should hold myself content to dwell with it alone to the end of my own days, though I suppose this causes you some concern for me. You wrote of our father remarrying in less than a year, I think, in your kindness, to assure me it would be no disrespect to Lucille were I to do the same. He was younger than I, and ourselves much littler, when he and Maggie were wed. Even were I of a mind to take another wife, there are but a few unmarried ladies dwelling nearby, only a widow or two who I should not think suitable due to age or temperament. The children are mostly old enough to see to the running of the household, and where there might yet be want of a mother's hand, Amelia has supplied that of eldest sister with such grace and gentleness as would have much pleased Lucille. You should not think even me helpless in these matters, Dear Sister. When Mother was ailing, was it not I who let you suck my little finger while I rocked you to sleep, cooked porridge for the rest of us, read stories aloud, and yes, even combed and braided my little sister's hair! Of course you would not remember yourself, but I assure you it is the truth, and our siblings will bear me up should you doubt me.

You also asked if I might now return to England. The answer, Dear Sister, is no. As I have written, the land is at last yielding us some profit, and I have hopes our continued industry and determination will see us to greater, though still modest, prosperity in the coming harvests. In any event, it must be some years before I should have the means for us all to cross the Atlantic again, even were I to wish it so, and I do not. Rather, it pleases my heart the children have set down little roots of their own here, like the tenderest of carrots in early summer, and I would not now pull them from this earth.

I confess I, too, in spite of all the losses and hardships we have endured, have grown to love this soil. When we first alighted from the ship in Montreal, the thought came to me I should never set foot on such a vessel again, nor suffer the reeking ports and grey seas I had so come to despise. The fiercest of prairie blizzards could not change my heart. Those dark waters that took our Father and Mother to their early deaths and lured my beloved Henry to the farthest reaches of the globe only to drown him, I should never again take their salty stench into my nostrils, nor bear their fetid touch on my skin.

I have instead discovered a new ocean, one of blue skies and swaying gold and green. I have discovered my home. Of course you should always be welcomed with joy and warmth in any home of mine, Dear Sister, should you and yours ever be moved by some calling in your hearts to join us. On many a dark eve I have placed a candle in my window with a thought to you, perhaps at that very moment climbing from your bed to glimpse the same stars disappearing below your horizon that now rise over ours. Often now I recall the years when you and I and our siblings shared table and bed. I think on the small rooms that once contained the whole of our family, and how strange it seems to me that our children are separated by a vast ocean and hardly acquainted, and our grandchildren never likely to meet. I suppose it must be that they too will venture forth someday, to search out their own homes under these boundless heavens.

Your most affectionate and devoted brother,
J.M.B.

"The Emigrants" originally appeared in *PRISM International.*

Skin to Skin
by Martha Miller

Lois and I are fighting again. I stick around longer than usual, trying to get the last word, and start out late. There's new snow on top of dirty old snow. We can't smoke in the center, so I smoke hurriedly on the walk over. At the corner, I look back at my lone tracks and pull my red coat together against a gust of wind. The sky is gunmetal gray; big billowy clouds are heavy with more snow.

Someone has shoveled the walk, and I stomp my feet all the way up the cleaned-off steps. Inside, I throw my red coat on the floor next to my chair, kick off my wet tennis shoes and draw my feet up under me. Group hasn't started yet. Anatole and Paul are talking, probably about sex. That's all these boys think about. Tim is on the couch, sideways, looking out the window behind him. He's an old guy; out of work—like most of us. His partner of thirty years died last spring. Two suicide attempts since then. I like him, but don't know how to tell him. He reminds me of my dad. My real dad.

I start the chair rocking with quick little bounces back and forth.

I staked out the olive green rocker after Kenney died. We all thought Kenney was going to make it this last time.

He was barely symptomatic, a KS lesion from time to time, you know, a little weight loss. Then boom. He gets pneumonia. Two, three days he's gone. The old nun cried. None of the group did, except that damn Cinnamon who cries over everything.

Cinnamon looks right at me. "How you doin,' Miss Thang?" he says.

"Just great," I say. "Where's Peggy?"

"New meat today," he says, as if that explains everything.

"This group is too fluid," says Tim. "We get a trust level built and somebody comes in, or somebody dies. I'm tired of losing people and tired of introductions, and I hate telling my story to new people. Hell, half of them never come back."

I decide right then and there that I'm not going to like the new guy, and say, "Damn right!" Tim smiles at me a little.

Cinnamon ignores us. He says, "We were all new once. Besides, if we made more people feel welcome they might come back a second time."

I turn to Tim to roll my eyes or something, but he's looking out the window again. Alone in our defense, I tell Cinnamon, "Welcoming people to this group is like greeting people at a thirty car pile up."

"What a clever simile," he responds in a tone that tells me he didn't think it was clever at all.

I say, "New guys just take one look at us and know where they're headed. That's why they don't come back."

"Well, thank the goddess we didn't scare *you* off," quips Cinnamon.

I don't answer.

Ten after four, Peggy comes in with the new guy. Except it isn't a guy. She's blonde, and looks like I should look for my age. I tell people I got forty-eight years of living into twenty-eight years of life. Good thing too, considering. The new girl's dressed nice: Doc Martens, light stone-washed jeans, a pink shaker sweater, two gold chains—not the flashy kind, but thin and fragile. I decide she's not one of us—probably a volunteer grad student or an intern. They come once in a while. The first time someone says fuck, suck or asshole, they quit. I don't want her in the group anyway. I've been the only female. The boys are used to me. I like it that way.

Peggy is the counselor. She's been here for six months. That's longer than most others. No one knows anything about her personal life, but her stocky, square build and short, short hair look masculine to me. Put a chambray shirt and a black vest on her, and she could have her pick of femmes. Today she wears a gray blazer and a black skirt. She sits in her usual flowery arm chair, and the blond sits on the couch next to Tim. I know he doesn't care for this, but he smiles politely. Old queens have the best manners.

Peggy says, "We have someone new today. Group, this is Crystal. Let's start with introductions." She turns to Cinnamon, a good place to start since he loves introductions.

He sits up straight in his chair, wiggling his black ass a little in the process. "My name is Cinnamon," he says. "Actually, that's my stage name." He flutters his hands in the air and smiles showing his huge white teeth. His face is thin, shaped like a dark brown horse. I've heard his story a hundred times and tune it out while I watch the new woman. She's looking right at Cinnamon, listening intently. There's a wrinkle between her brows, like it's hard work. Finally Cinnamon ends with, "James died three years ago, February. The ground was frozen solid; we had to wait a month to bury his ashes."

"Thanks, Cinnamon," says Peggy. Then she fucking turns to me! "How about you next?"

"Name's Peaches," I say.

Peggy waits a few seconds, and then says, "Can you tell Crystal about yourself, Peaches?"

I decide to let her have it. "I kicked heroin five years ago in prison. I used to support me and my boyfriend's habit hustling. He died, and I got arrested. Inside I hooked up with Lois. Since we got out, we share a place. I guess I'm a dyke now. I'm racially mixed, five-three and weigh ninety-eight pounds. Don't ask me what race, and don't ask me nothin' about my name." I fold my arms across my chest and shut my mouth.

There is a short silence. Peggy is probably trying to decide whether to press it or go on. I hear the phone ring up front. The nun answers. She's a good old girl. Not like the others. Nuns, I mean.

Tim starts talking, and Peggy looks at him surprised. "Welcome to our group, Crystal." He lays his hand on her arm gently. I can see her stiffen. He says, "I mean no offense, but I don't feel like telling my life story today. I will take Peaches' lead. I am Caucasian, fifty-one years old, five-foot nine and weigh 165 pounds on a good day. I used to work for a bank. Now I don't."

Skipping over Crystal, Paul goes next. He finishes with, "I'm not going to tell you my weight, or my age." This breaks the tension and we all laugh, including Peggy. Paul is actually the youngest. He started the protease inhibitor several months ago and no longer has severe symptoms. His parents can keep him on their insurance policy as long as he takes classes and is under the age of twenty-three. He is desperate to find a job because his time is running out.

Anatole has been positive for fourteen years. I think he looks down on the rest of us who are symptomatic. I've noticed with the guys there's this gulf between the virus and the disease; it's how they categorize themselves. Anatole quickly makes it clear that he has never been sick. Then he uses the ticking time bomb analogy; all of his friends from fourteen years ago are dead; his life could blow up at any moment. Anatole has an MBA, but works for a temp agency. Every time someone finds out about his HIV status, the placement abruptly ends. He can't get disability because he isn't sick, and he's running out of places he can work.

We've been around the circle and Peggy turns back to Crystal. Crystal sits up straight and kind of flushes. She says, "I've been positive for two years that I know of. I found out when I was pregnant with my youngest son. He died six months ago. I just lost my husband." She looks like she's going to cry, and that makes me mad. What if we all started crying? Where would it end? "I—I'm not sure I belong here," she finishes.

I wonder what the hell that means. But in the short silence that follows, I know. We've got our first innocent victim, and she's in the unique position of thinking she doesn't deserve to die. I stare at my tennis shoes that are making a puddle and feel rage bubble up inside me. The room is too warm. I want to talk about my problems, about the fight with Lois. I want to find out what's going on with Tim. Instead, we're going to have to spend the session convincing Suzie Homemaker that she belongs here.

Tim seems to be looking at my shoes, too, as he starts to talk. "Everyone in this group has lost loved ones. Sometimes we are a grief support group as much as anything. If you decide you belong here, we can help you with that."

"You misunderstand me," Crystal protests.

I say, "I doubt it." Break is forty minutes away, but that will be the last thing I contribute. I halfway listen, halfway pass the time going over the fight with Lois and marking the minutes until I can get outside to smoke. There are long silences, followed by Peggy's efforts to pull things together. Cinnamon, who's the counselor's pet, is the only one who shares anything. The rest of us, including Crystal, have withdrawn.

At five-thirty I get back into my wet tennis shoes, pull on the red coat and look for Tim. He has followed the new woman into the kitchen to get coffee. He's trying to talk to her. Paul doesn't smoke and Anatole is trying to quit. I have to share the porch with Cinnamon.

Dark clouds are breaking up in the west and the sun is setting over the tops of the buildings along Fifth Street, outlining them with a medley of pink and gold and gray. I stand against the building in a corner out of the cold wind. Cinnamon leans against the porch rail and looks at me. "How come you're so quiet?"

"Am I? I hadn't noticed."

He cups his hands around his lighter. Soon steam from his breath and cigarette smoke float in the air around his face. A gust of wind blows it all away. He looks at the sky.

"That sunset sure is pretty," he says. "Reminds me of summer flowers."

"Are you nuts?" I say. "It reminds me that it will be dark when we get out of here, and I have to walk home freezing my ass, wondering who will come out of the next alley at me."

"Want me to walk with you?" he asks.

I toss the cigarette down and step on it. "I got enough to worry about without taking care of your ass too." I go back inside, slamming the door behind me. The group room is still empty. I look at my rocker, the wet spots on the floor. If I have to do this for another hour, I know I'll explode. I can see brains dripping from the ceiling, a bony stump where my head used to be. At first I tell myself that I will have another cigarette on the back steps. I walk through the kitchen smiling at the others. When the door shuts behind me, I start to run. Tears sting my eyes, then burn cold on my cheeks. My coat flies open.

I sit on the landing between the second and third floor for a long time, smoking. Lois isn't expecting me home for a while. I can hear the floor screech as she walks around up there. She's got music on, and she's humming with it. I can't remember what the fight was about. Another one of my black moods brought on by generic cigarettes, cockroaches in the kitchen and day-time television. I can smell fried onions and potatoes from the supper she's cooking. Lois is a big girl. Likes her food. It don't matter to me. We all find our paths to oblivion.

Then the door up there opens and yellow light from our living room falls across the top steps. Lois is saying, "Jesus

Christ! I thought the building was on fire. Get your bony ass up here, girl, and give me one of them cigarettes!"

Lois talks like southern white trash. Her mama was originally from some little town in the hills of Arkansas. Lois' step-daddy had his way with her, just like mine did me. I've known other women, especially in prison, who've had this common experience. To the last one, they are either overweight like Lois or underweight like me. Most of them are crack or meth addicts, twenty-years-old looking fifty.

I give her the smoke I just lit and scoot past her into the warm apartment. Lois has covered the windows with plastic and keeps the gas oven going most of the time. She's good at some things. The TV is on and the table is set for one.

"Want a plate?" she asks.

"I'm not hungry."

"Come on, Peaches, you got to eat once in a while."

I see a thick hamburger dripping with grease and half a plate of brown potatoes. She's got two cans of Coke open. None of it looks good.

"Had a big lunch," I say.

She says, "Liar," but that's as far as it goes.

She brings me a beer and I stare in the direction of the television while she smacks her lips behind me. Today's paper is spread across the floor. She's been looking for a job again. My disability and her township barely keep us going. Lois' parole officer got her into one of those training programs where she learned typing and computers. She had hopes for a while. But, prospective employers see her last stint of employment was in the kitchen at Dwight Correctional Center, and they aren't impressed.

I turn. Her fork stops in midair. I say, "I'm sorry."

She smiles. "About time."

Later, in bed, I roll close to her, slide my hand down her round belly and work my fingers between her folds. She's hot and slippery. I move my fingers in a circular motion, pressing slowly. She spreads her knees beneath the blankets, and her arms envelop me. I straddle her and slide down. I love the taste of her cunt. In the old days I could come just thinking about it. When I sense she is close, I change the motion, teasing her. I slide three fingers inside. She is pleading with me by the time she finishes.

I lie behind her spoon fashion and holding her while she trembles.

"Let me do you," she says without turning.

"I already got it, babe," I tell her.

"Liar," she says.

It's been like this since the new anti-depressant. I don't feel sexual. I don't feel anything but angry and depressed. Sometimes the boys talk about fear that they will never have sex again. Losing sex is like losing a limb. No, worse—it's like dying. Kenney went through it. He used to wonder if he would ever have another relationship or ever get laid again. We tried to reassure him, but it turned out he was right. Others, like Paul and Anatole, are compulsive about it. They can't get enough. Sooner or later the medications will render them impotent. They know it's coming. They'll call it erectile dysfunction for a while and ask their doctors for the drugs that aging baby boomers use. But eventually even Viagra will fail because sex is more than an erection.

The nun calls me Monday morning and asks how I am. I tell her I wasn't feeling good Friday and I needed to leave early. She doesn't confront me, but doesn't let me off the hook either.

"We need you in the group, Peaches, more than ever now. Crystal needs you."

"There wasn't any woman there for me when I started," I say. "I don't like her."

"Give her a chance," says the old nun. "For me."

A professional counselor could never do this. But nuns can do anything. They are especially good with guilt. "Well, I didn't say I quit. I just wasn't feeling good."

"Then you'll be back next Friday night?"

"Sure," I say. "Wouldn't miss it."

She hesitates. "Talk to Crystal when you can."

I tell her, "Okay. First chance I get."

But no one sees the new woman for a long time. I figure it's just as well.

In April Lois gets a job at Howard Johnson's working three to eleven. I miss her in the evenings and find myself taking change from her tip jar, walking six blocks to the restaurant and buying endless cups of coffee. Lois complains that she could seat paying customers in my spot. But she keeps pouring the coffee and talking to me during the slow periods. Once or twice I stay right to the end of her shift.

That's where I am one rainy Thursday night when I see Crystal and her kid. Of course, they are in non-smoking all the way across the room. She's lost some weight since last winter and looks like she has a cold or something. The kid is restless. Crystal is having a hard time.

I tell Lois to fill up one of those balloons that they give to kids, and I take it over. I lean across the booth and say, "Here ya' go, buddy. Knock yourself out."

Crystal says, "Peaches."

I smile at her. I wasn't sure she'd remember me. "How you been, Crystal?"

"Not so good," she admits. "In and out of the hospital. New medications. You know."

I nod. I do know; I been given last rites twice already.

The kid is about five or six. He busts the first balloon pretty fast and Lois is quick to bring another, along with some color crayons and a paper place mat for him to draw on. Crystal starts to give Lois her order, then turns to me and says, "Will you join me?"

I jerk my thumb. "I got coffee over there."

"Well, bring it over."

Lois gives me a strange look as I go back and get my coffee cup.

The kid sits next to Crystal, the top of his tongue sticking out of the corner of his mouth while he tries to do a maze. There is an awkward silence that Crystal finally breaks. "You been in the group long?"

"A year and a half," I say.

"Were you angry with me the day I was there?"

I sip the tepid coffee, then say, "Probably, but don't take it personal. I'm mad most of the time. We all are."

Crystal says, "I can relate to that." Then Lois is there setting a hamburger and fries in front of the kid, and a large salad in front of Crystal.

Lois refills my coffee and their water. As soon as she's gone I lean forward and say, "What are *you* mad at?" I figure it is probably me, for messing up her chance at the group.

"I'm mad at the whole world," she says.

I slap my palm on the table and say, "Good start."

She smiles, then turns to the kid and tells him to use his fork for the French fries. It's really none of my business, but I say, "Let him do what he wants. Life is short."

She doesn't let him eat with his fingers, but nods to let me know that she thinks I'm right about life.

"Come back to the group," I say. "Us girls got to stick together."

"You don't strike me as the type who needs anyone," she says, shaking her head. "Anyway, I can't. I'd have to get a sitter. I want to spend every minute with my son."

How far am I supposed to go for a nun? I take one last shot. "What good is time with him when you're always mad?"

She sighs. "I guess I could try."

I am amazed it is this easy. Maybe she wants to come back, after all.

Crystal puts down her fork and pushes the salad away. "So, how did you get infected?"

"That's a very personal question," I say grimly.

"I'm sorry. Forget I asked."

I shrug. "Tainted needles. Prostitution. I'm not sure. I did a lot of high risk things before I went to prison."

"I remember now," she says.

"So, how about you?"

She looks like she's not going to tell me. Then she blurts it out. "I was married to a Baptist minister who saw prostitutes when he traveled."

"That's tough," I say, wondering if she thinks I am one of them.

"Edwin and I separated after the baby died. I was so angry I couldn't look at him; then he died last November."

"Were you mad at him because of AIDS, or the infidelity?" I ask.

"Edwin had a rough childhood," she says softly. "One foster home after another. Abuse of all kinds. He was a strong man, but he didn't have any boundaries with sex. I had forgiven him before. I *did* understand, in a way. I loved the way he had pulled himself up by the bootstraps. Sometimes I think the person who abused him is really the mass murderer."

I think about Kenney and the others who have a history of incest and abuse—Lois and me—those women in prison. Maybe there is a connection. "What do you mean by sexual boundaries?" I ask.

She looks at me as if she's wondering if I can understand. Then she looks at the kid, and I know I'll have to find out about it some other time. I sip on my coffee. She picks up her fork again, takes tiny bites and chews them for a long time. She makes a face when she swallows.

I almost wish I could drop it, but I try again. "So, do you blame your husband for AIDS? I mean if you understand about the prostitutes…"

She angrily drops her fork. "You bet I blame him!"

"What about the abuser-murderer?" I demand.

She narrows her eyes. "Did you bring all this up just to unload your shit on me?"

I'm too angry to stop. "Your husband went outside your marriage and got infected. So AIDS is his punishment?"

"He gave it to me," she raises her voice. The kid next to her looks scared. "He gave it to our baby."

"Right." It comes out very loud. "You and that baby are innocent victims—I almost forgot!" This was what pissed me off before. It hasn't changed. But why should it? Our whole damn culture thinks this way.

She looks at me squarely and says, "There *are* innocent victims, you know."

I don't remember standing, but I am on my feet. "There aren't any other kind," I shout at her, then turn and leave, without even saying good-bye to Lois.

I am surprised when the next afternoon Crystal shows up at group. I don't talk to her, but Cinnamon falls all over himself to make her welcome. I decide I won't talk to him either.

The nun comes out on the porch while I am on break smoking. "Crystal said that you ran into her and asked her to come back."

I won't look in the nun's eyes. I just nod.

"You did a good thing, Peaches. Thank you."

I look at her then, wondering what she would say if she had the whole story.

Back in group, Paul is upset because his insurance company told him he has reached his lifetime maximum and canceled his policy. He can't afford the protease inhibitors on his own, and has been told that they may not work for him if he stops, then starts again.

There was a program that used to pay for my AZT, but then there were funding cuts. Whenever my doctor has samples of anything, he gives them to me.

Tim says, "The AIDS crisis will never be over as long as people can't afford the miracle drugs."

"How much do your meds cost, anyway?" Crystal asks.

I jerk my head around. I had forgotten she was there.

Paul tells her that his cocktail, and everything else, runs about eighteen hundred a month. I wonder how she got this far and didn't know. She turns pale.

Peggy interrupts. "The church provides us with some funds. We try to connect people with any funds available: Medicaid, Compassionate Use, experimental treatments, that sort of thing. We can get meals taken to your apartment. We can get sick people into the Buddy System. We have some housing, not a lot. But we work hard to keep people out of nursing homes or, or…"

"Off the street," I finish for her.

"My god," Crystal says softly.

We say nothing. The nun in the reception area is quiet. The faint creaking of my rocking chair is the only noise in the center.

In the months that follow Cinnamon takes up with a new man. Crystal wastes a lot of time feeling sorry for herself because she'll never see her little boy grow up. Like she's the only one in the room who ever lost anything. As the days of summer grow hot and long, Lois and I are fighting with a new intensity. My nerves are shot.

Paul has moved back with his parents in Chicago, and Tim's depression is worse than ever. The disease has found his weakness. He let his guard down. Peggy accuses him of stopping his medications. He does not deny this. I think of all the methods of suicide, this has to be the worst. I've seen others scream in pain, lose their minds, lie in their own shit. A gun would be faster and hurt less. I catch him after group and try to tell him I'll help him. There are dark circles around his eyes; his skin is not the right color. Close up I can smell death on him.

"You know," I say. "If you're in pain, I still have street connections."

He shakes his head slowly and says, "Thanks, I'm okay."

On nights I can't sleep, I sit on the second story roof, which extends outside our bedroom window and smoke. I watch the wind move the leaves in the tree tops and sometimes I feel a gentle breeze. The roof slants down in either direction; the shingles are rough and still hold some heat from the sun. Lois comes home later and later. Since she's got money again, she is drinking more and going to the bar after work with a new friend. Terror pounds in my throat until I can't swallow my own spit. The clouds drift past the moon, and I wait, flipping cigarette butts, watching them arch in the air and leave a trail of sparks in the darkness. The night I climb back through the window and find her packing, I know the wait has ended, and it's almost a relief.

I don't cry when Lois moves her things out. She says from the doorway, "The rent is paid until the first. That should give you time to get next month together or find another place."

We both know I can't get next month's rent together. I say, "Thanks."

She sets the last box in the hallway and turns.

"This new woman know you got it?" I ask.

Lois screws up her face in anger. "No!" she says. "And I ain't gonna' tell her. I'm not sick. I may never get sick."

That makes sense to me. "It was good while it lasted," I say.

She stands there like she wants to say something, but in the end she just closes the door.

Ironically, the next Friday, Crystal is complaining about living alone and handling the kid by herself. She's tired all the time. When I say Lois and I have broken up, Peggy suggests that Crystal and I could help each other out. Anatole jumps in like an enthusiastic matchmaker. I turn to Crystal, who has the couch she usually shares with Tim to herself. She is looking at me. We are both horrified.

The nun stops me as I start toward the door at break. She says, "Tim is in the hospital."

"Is it bad?"

She looks at me a minute, then says, "Yes."

"Which one?" I ask. "What room?"

She writes down the numbers on a yellow Post-it pad. I stuff the sticky sheet in my pocket and go outside to smoke.

The room stinks. Tim has the look of someone who has been sleeping for a long time—one of those deep sleeps where you don't roll over, or wake up when your bladder is full. There's an arrangement of flowers on the window sill; Cinnamon is sitting next to them, reading. I almost leave. Then I remember that there might not be another chance, and I make myself go in.

Cinnamon looks up and says, "How you doin,' Peaches?"

"He okay?" I ask.

Cinnamon shakes his head. "His sister was up here awhile ago. She says they're taking the body back to Indiana."

"So what?"

"So, another memorial service with no body, that's what," Cinnamon says. "It's like our friends just disappear. There's no closure."

"I've had enough closure for five people."

"What they do with your boyfriend when he died?"

"None of your damn business," I say. Cinnamon always wants to talk about feelings. I figure you open a door to things when you talk about them. I don't want to feel.

He won't drop it. "Did you see him? Did he have a funeral?"

"Last I saw him, we were running; the police shot him. His parents took care of everything while I was in jail." I can say this without tears. I just speak evenly. The thing is, sometimes I can't remember what he looked like. I try to, but it's gone.

"Was there a funeral?" Cinnamon seems genuinely interested.

I shrug. "They let me go. This county matron sat next to me. I wouldn't let her see me cry. Brian's parents refused to look at me. The matron called my friends thugs and cuffed me in front of them."

"But you saw him in the coffin?"

"Yeah."

Cinnamon sighs. "All I'm saying is—it makes a difference."

I move close to the bed. Tim is pale and very thin. There are tubes going in and out of him everywhere. I touch his arm. It's too cold, and I pull the white blanket up to his shoulders. "How long he been like this?" I ask.

"Three days."

"Hell, he's gone already. He wants to die. Why don't they just unhook him?"

Cinnamon doesn't answer. I sit in the hard chair and Cinnamon leans back on the turquoise vinyl. Outside the room there are voices; two women are looking for a room number. I feel hypnotized by the beeping machine. Cinnamon is staring at Tim.

"You two know each other long?" I ask.

"I met him in group," Cinnamon says. "We'd both lost our partners."

My eyes have drifted to the flower arrangement. "You bring those?" I ask.

Cinnamon nods, then stands and starts fluffing Tim's pillow.

I look at the beeping machine, and then make myself look at Tim.

Cinnamon is stroking Tim's gray hair. I walk around the bed and motion for him to let me close. He nods and backs away. I work my arm under Tim's neck. He is light, almost like nothing. His breath is bad. There's a tube going in his nose. I get as close to his ear as I can and whisper, "I always liked you best."

Cinnamon takes my hand and gently pulls me away. He guides me into the hallway and kind of leans against the wall. "Not everyone has the courage to go on," he says. "Especially when they're alone."

I nod, and suddenly I am talking about Lois.

Cinnamon seems to be studying the floor tiles. When I finish, he says, "You had dinner?"

"Not hungry," I answer.

"Lois leave you any groceries?"

"A ton," I lie.

"Well, I'm hungry. I want to talk," he says. "I mean, you been left and so have I. Maybe we could cry on each other's shoulders over some Chinese food."

I hate Chinese. I'm broke. "I left my money in my other pants," I say.

"Let me buy." He won't let go of it.

Outside, the sun is low; it must be after eight. We walk two blocks to a little tavern that serves Chinese food. The place is almost empty, except for two guys at the bar watching a baseball game. There's no one in the dining room. The guy who takes our order is young and Asian. Cinnamon watches him each time he brings something and walks away.

"So," I say when we both have a cup of very strong tea in front of us. "What happened to your new love?"

"What always happens," he says, looking at his cup. "I told him I was positive when I met him. He was too. It seemed like a match made in heaven. Then he found out that I got sick from time to time. He accused me of lying. Said I didn't tell him I had AIDS."

"Did you?" I ask.

"I said I was *positive,* and I am."

"You misled him," I say. "Which is better than Lois. She didn't even tell her new woman about her HIV. She says she might not ever get sick. Maybe she's right. There's all that stuff about lesbians not being able to transmit the virus through sex."

Cinnamon empties his tea cup and pours more from the pot. "There are too many things that no one knows," he says. "I always tell my lovers. I am careful about their protection. Then this latest guy, Max, takes me in his mouth anyway. I have this moment of panic. I want what he's doing so much. He knows about me…"

"Not everything," I cut in.

"Not everything," Cinnamon admits. "But being touched is a powerful thing. I remember the days when I took skin to skin for granted. I may be sick, but I am human, too."

"You are supposed to play it safe even if you are both positive," I say, reminding him of the many different strains of the virus. But, I know what he means. We are all human.

Cinnamon holds up a hand to quiet me just as the waiter delivers my cashew chicken. The plate is heaping. There is a separate bowl for rice. The dinner probably weighs more than I do.

"You got more than me," Cinnamon says when the Asian boy is gone.

I look at his sweet and sour pork. He's right. I say, "I think your boyfriend is straight."

Cinnamon grins and starts stuffing the dark orange chunks of meat in his mouth.

I haven't eaten all day. I had some tomato soup and a bologna sandwich at the bread line yesterday. The Chinese food actually smells good, and we both eat in silence for a while. I dig out all the chunks of chicken and the cashews. I don't like half raw vegetables. I soak up some of the juices with the white rice. The plate is halfway empty when I stop and break open my fortune cookie. It says, "Good news will come in the mail." I happen to know that good news comes by phone and bad news comes by mail. I eat the cookie.

"Want mine?" Cinnamon asks.

"It's *your* fortune," I say.

He pops the cookie open. "Mine says, you will have a comfortable old age." He throws back his head and laughs.

I don't know what else to do, so I laugh with him.

Then we are quiet, and I say, "I know where my future is if something don't change. I'm going to come home some night and the landlord will have a padlock on the door."

Cinnamon looks at me seriously. He shakes his dark, bony finger. "You don't ever have to sleep in the street long as I got a recliner."

"No couch?"

"Honey, I live in one room."

"Thanks," I tell him. I pick up my fork and start moving the vegetables around on my plate. There's no more chicken, and I try something that looks like a baby ear of corn. It doesn't taste much like corn. It doesn't taste like anything.

"Know what you oughta do?" Cinnamon is shaking that finger again. "You oughta approach Crystal. She has a huge place and is having trouble managing it alone. She likes you."

"She's straight."

"Oh, I know that. I mean she likes you as a fellow member of the club. She's got this idea you're stronger than the rest of us because you're madder than the rest of us."

I look at him then. I never cared much for Cinnamon. I see now, he don't hold that against me. His hands are trembling slightly. "You okay?" I ask.

"It's been a long day. I just need to get home."

"I'll walk with you."

"No," he protests. "Then you'll have to get back alone."

"I insist," I say and ignore his protests.

Friday, Peggy announces that Tim died the night before. We spend most of the group time on Crystal's money problems. She's on public aid now. She shops with food stamps. She can't afford her insurance premiums. I listen and try to imagine living with her. I can't.

At break I skip the cigarette and follow Crystal into the kitchen. She smiles at me and puts four coins in the Coke machine.

I say, "I've been shopping with food stamps since I was a little kid. It don't bother me."

She hangs her head and says, "I suppose I shouldn't be so arrogant."

"Well," I say. "That's not the most humiliating thing that you got ahead of you. But I understand. It's like you've sunk one more level."

She meets my eyes, and says, "Exactly."

"Let me help you out."

"Oh, I couldn't."

I take a deep breath and it feels like all my wind comes out when I say, "Please."

I look up and see the old nun standing in the doorway. She is smiling. She claps both her hands together and says, "This is wonderful. Oh, I am so happy." She lays one hand on my shoulder and says to Crystal, "I have been so worried about this one. She's never been close to anyone in the group. I know the two of you living under the same roof is God's plan. There's so much you can teach each other."

I watch the color rise in Crystal's face. Her eyes are wide as she turns to me. I feel the weight of the nun's hand on my shoulder.

I am trapped.

Crystal smiles suddenly. "There's a futon in Edwin's study. I been using it as a junk room, but we could clean it out. You do need a place to stay, don't you?"

The nun speaks up for me. "Of course she does."

I stand there quiet while Crystal and the nun make plans. It's either this or Cinnamon's recliner, I tell myself.

At the end of group, we say a prayer for Tim, and then Peggy makes an announcement about a Memorial Service at the MCC church.

As it turns out, Crystal gives me a ride home that night. I ask her to come up for instant coffee, and we find a padlock on my apartment door.

"I don't believe they really do this to people," she says.

I admit, "I'm two months behind."

She runs down the steps, and climbs back up a few minutes later with a jack handle. We both take as much as we can carry, up and down until neither of us can make another trip. I sleep on the futon that night, soundly.

We have things to work out, the most important of which is, I smoke. After Crystal tries to get me to quit, she shrugs her shoulders and goes out to the garage. She sets a webbed lawn chair next to the back steps and gives me the lid of a big pickle jar for an ashtray. That is my smoking place. The house is three bedrooms on a slab. The smallest bedroom is the study. It's a mess with all my things and some of Edwin's. The three of us share one bathroom, but every time I feel resentful about it, I conjure up the image of the padlock.

The kid hates me. Crystal forces him to be polite, but his feelings are clear. I don't care much for him, but I can see the advantages of getting along. I never had a kid. Nobody I was ever with had a kid. I had six brothers and sisters, all older. I feel out of my element. Another drawback of our living arrangement is when I need to talk to the group about home or my roommates, I can't. Crystal is there.

I get in the habit of staying up late, watching T.V. Commercial time I go out on the back steps and smoke. I like the time alone. I am watching a baseball game one night when the kid gets up to pee. He doesn't flush. He comes into the living room and looks at the T.V. He is in his under shorts. There's a pee dribble about the size of a quarter right in the middle of the front. His legs are skinny and his blonde hair is standing up in back.

I ignore him. Actually, I forget he's there. Then his reedy voice startles me. "My dad was going to teach me how to play baseball when I was big enough."

I look at him; he hasn't taken his eyes off the game. I think about the father who won't be there to teach him anything. I think about Crystal who is now symptomatic and probably won't see him through his tenth year. Maybe they'll come up with new meds. She's white and she's straight. She has a chance. Finally I say, "Baseball ain't hard.

You just got to remember to keep your eyes open and on the ball."

He's twirling his hair. He does this so often and so intently that sometimes Crystal has to cut out the knots. It reminds me of the comfort I found sucking my thumb until I was almost nine years old. I quit when I found cigarettes. The kid says, "I got a ball."

"Where?" I ask.

He runs off to his room and takes so long I figure he's down for the night. But later he comes back with a rubber ball that looks like a baseball. He hands it to me.

I scoot from the chair to the floor and spread my legs out wide. I tell the kid to sit opposite me. "We'll start just rolling it," I tell him. So, we roll the ball back and forth. Then we bounce it. It doesn't bounce high on the carpet. The kid is smiling. I can see a space where a front tooth is out and a tooth next to the space is half grown in.

I say, "You've done this before."

"I have not!"

"Well, you're pretty good," I say, and I surprise him by tossing the ball without bouncing it. He closes his eyes, but somehow catches it.

I hear the T.V. announcer say it's the top of the ninth. I wonder what time it is. The kid is laughing, trying to throw the ball without bouncing. He makes some wild tosses and more than once I fall over, stretching to save a lamp. We must have gotten pretty loud because when I fall over backwards catching a pitch that is too high, I see the hem of Crystal's blue night gown. Suddenly everything is quiet.

"Peaches is teaching me to throw," the kid finally says.

"It's late now," says Crystal. "You two can play tomorrow."

The kid stands up and steps over me. "Night, Peaches," he says.

I scoot back up on the couch. The television ball game is over, and I don't know who won. I put my head in my hands and say, "I'm sorry. I guess I just got carried away."

Crystal places her hand on my shoulder and says, "Don't apologize. I should be thanking you." She touches the skin on my neck. Involuntarily I nuzzle my head against her palm. She jerks her hand away. I hadn't meant to do it. I'm sure I will be in the street by tomorrow.

Crystal drops on the couch next to me, but I won't look at her. "We need to relax," she says. She reaches to the end table, opens a drawer and extracts a small metal container that once held Christmas cookies. She sets it on the arm of my chair and pops it open. Inside are papers, a one hitter, roach clips and a baggie containing about a half an ounce of pot.

I am too surprised to speak.

"I need this little pipe," she says, "because I never mastered rolling them. Can you roll? I prefer it that way."

I take the canister and set to work.

"It's medicinal," she says suddenly.

"Honey, you don't have to sell me on this," I answer. I roll a fat one. What the hell?

We light up and pass the joint back and forth. For a woman who doesn't even smoke cigarettes, she does pretty well. I can feel the stuff relax me. It's got to be sinsemilla. I think about the food stamps and insurance premiums. "Where'd you get this?" I ask.

"This house is the parsonage," says Crystal. "The church is behind us, on the corner. When we split, Edwin wanted me to stay here. When he died, the church insisted I stay on. You probably won't believe this, but the Ladies Tuesday Night Bible Study group scored this pot."

I have been holding my breath. I spit it out and start gagging. "Oh God, I *want* to believe that one."

We both start laughing. We smoke the joint down, and I slip a roach clip on it. In the end I am sucking in the smoke from the last ember.

Crystal lightly slurs her words. "You know, there's something I've been dying to ask you."

"What?"

"How did you end up with the name Peaches?"

"My mother has very dark skin," I say. "She told me when I was born my skin was the color of peaches and cream."

"You said not to ask about your mixed race. Does it bother you?"

It's then I remember the first night of group. It never occurred to me that I would eventually answer those questions. "It's just too complicated," I say, but I find myself telling her the whole story in a controlled monotone. "My mother was mostly black, some Mexican. My father was Italian. I got six older half brothers and sisters; we all got different fathers. Mine come back for me once. My mama cleaned me up, made me a new dress and bought brand new white socks. She braided my hair and made me sit still all morning. When he come in he threw his arms around me and hollered, 'This is my baby.' I snuggled into his neck. It smelled nice and clean. He was with his new wife. When she saw my yellow skin and nappy hair, she pulled my father out the door. My things had been packed to go with them, and my mother cried. At the time I figured it was because she didn't want me. Looking back, I know I was wrong."

"How?" asks Crystal.

"My step-daddy was already after my older sisters. It was just a matter of time before he got around to me. She saw my real father as a way out. I found out later she called him to come get me because she knew."

"She should have thrown the bastard in jail," says Crystal.

I shrug. "He had a job."

She nods. These days she has a new understanding of poverty. She has taken in a room mate, bought groceries with food stamps, made choices between MasterCard payments and medicine, but she'd never been poor enough to ignore the abuse of a child.

We talk for a while about group and the guys. We talk about Tim, and I tell her how he reminded me of my father, silver hair, broad shoulders. I tell her about the hospital room, Cinnamon and the fortune cookies. I tell her why his latest fling ended, and our conversation about skin to skin. I'm not heading anywhere. I just like talking to her.

She goes in the kitchen and brings back a bag of cheese curls. We eat and talk some more. When I roll the second joint, I get that damn cheese stuff all over the paper. It has a strange smell as it burns. She hands me a beer, and I see she has one open too.

"You know," she says. "I really understand what Cinnamon means by skin to skin. I don't miss sex. But I do miss that grown-up human touching."

"Me too," I admit.

Crystal starts to cry. Amateur, I think, next she'll be puking. "You okay?"

She nods. "It's just all, so—" But she doesn't find the right words and lets it drop.

I feel like I ought to do something, but I don't know what. I pat her hand and say, "There, there." A straight man could have done better.

But she doesn't pull away, and I am left with my hand lying over hers. She turns and looks at me. "Would you like a back rub?"

Fear steps on my guts. I feel confused, but I nod slowly.

"Lie down on the floor." She gets up and staggers to the kitchen.

I stretch out on my belly and feel the soft carpet fibers tickle my nose. I am almost asleep when she returns, gets on her knees beside me, and says, "You'll have to take off your T-shirt."

I rise up, strip it off and lie back down. Now the rough carpet is tickling my nipples. She pours something warm on my back. "What is that?" I ask.

"Baby oil," she answers. "Edwin taught me this trick. I don't like to think where he learned it. It does feel good, doesn't it?"

I feel like I'm on a cloud. It is a most exquisite high. Her hands spread the warm oil across my back. She kneads my shoulders, firmly massaging my neck. I think of a back rub as short and sweet. But Crystal goes on and on.

"What is this?" she asks, touching my right side below my armpit.

"Herpes lesion," I say into the carpet, thinking the massage is surely over now.

"Does it hurt?"

"It hurt like hell at first, but it's healing," I manage to say.

She pours more warm oil and continues gently. I am in tears.

I don't know how long the massage lasts. She straddles my hips and works from that position for awhile. Finally she moves off me and stops. I roll over and look up at her. She nervously looks away from my breasts. I sit up, pull on my T-shirt, and say, "I'll rub your back now."

"I'm tired," she says.

"On your bed, then," I say. "When you fall asleep, I'll stop."

She stands and walks down the hall. I grab the baby oil and a towel and follow her. She leaves her bedroom door open, and I stand in the doorway while my eyes adjust to the dark. I can see her strip off her nightgown by the moonlight that falls through the only window. She is silhouetted against it: white glowing flesh and glistening golden hair. She slowly stretches across the covers on her belly.

The oil has cooled. I crawl on my knees across the huge bed. I kneel beside her, squeeze the stuff into my palm and wait to let it warm. Finally, I place my hand flat between her shoulders. She tries to hide it, but I feel her quiver. I rub the oil in circles, slowly. My fingers tingle with heat. When the oil covers her back, I straddle her hips and start gently kneading her shoulders. I think about Lois, the taste and the smell of her. I remember her round belly and soft breasts. I wonder if Crystal is thinking about Edwin. My hands slide effortlessly across her smooth skin. I feel relaxed by the repetitive motion. I hear her breathing slow and deep, and I don't ever want to stop.

Long after Crystal is asleep, and before I lie across the futon in Edwin's study, I go out to the webbed lawn chair to smoke. My T-shirt sticks to my back. My hands are slippery and smell of baby oil. I feel calm and satisfied.

I think about touching Crystal, and how it must be part of a powerful human hunger, how people have and will continue to risk their lives for it. And I know that isn't going to change. My libido is asleep, or dead, yet the touch of another human being is still the only thing that matters. I feel alive. Connected.

I look at the night sky. A dark, wispy cloud floats in front of the moon. Some great truth is right on the tip of my brain. It seems to me a person ought to understand life before they leave it. That's what old age is about. But the truth seems like long division, something I'll stand at the blackboard forever and never understand. I remember the nun, weeks ago, saying that Crystal and I could teach each other. But I am tired and a little too high. I stub my cigarette out and stand, thinking the puzzle will be there tomorrow. I just *got* to hold on to this piece I found tonight.

"Skin to Skin" originally appeared in the author's anthology *Skin to Skin: Erotic Lesbian Love Stories.*

A Can of Ice-Cold Sunkist Soda
by Van Newell

After graduating college I couldn't score a job interview so I ended up resuming my old gig as a lifeguard in Panama City Beach. Instead of a wooden high-chair style tower, I sat in a plastic chair that was pastel blue on top of a square ten by ten slab of concrete. Everyday I wore CVS brand sunblock that smelled like sugar cookies, cheap banana-colored sunglasses, a white "LIFEGUARD" shirt that was stained and a green fisherman's cap so my scalp wouldn't burn.

The waters of the Gulf of Mexico are more placid in northwest Florida than the waters of the Atlantic on the eastern part of the state. The waves are soft, fat, and slow, leisurely in their approach and arrivals. The riptides are mild annoyances at worst. My job as lifeguard was more helping parents chase down toddlers that were running on the sand rather than saving lives.

With my friends becoming certified financial planners and chemical engineers, I would have spent the whole summer in a depression if Dr. Fields had not laid down her towel near me. The book in her hand was a collection of the plays of Sophocles. I wondered what kind of person read that at the beach. I helped her set up her umbrella. Once she was situated, she poured herself a concoction that was equal parts Sunkist and Miller High Life into a red plastic cup.

She was thirty-four but her pixie haircut did not make her seem twelve years older than me. She had rusty brown hair and wore soccer shorts and a spaghetti-strap shirt. There were lines of skin on her kneecaps and calves that looked like surgery scars. Dr. Fields was the only woman on the beach not in a swimsuit.

Boredom sat in and I began to walk around to stretch my legs and I asked her if she was on vacation. She told me she had moved back to Panama City to teach at the community college. It turned out she had grown up here and we had actually graduated from the same high school.

During my third week on the job my brother Lee came to visit. He hated his job as a "vendor fulfillment coordinator" for a health care company in Macon, Georgia but he had been doing it long enough to accrue four weeks of vacation a year. Lee would get up early to play golf at the public course each morning and then he would bring lunch for me everyday from a grocery store deli. One day it was jerk chicken subs, the next it was turkey meatloaf, another was hardboiled eggs and collards. Even though I was nine years younger than Lee, he said he still missed doing the little things with me, like riding in the car together or going to see violent movies. With three daughters at home, he was fatigued from family life.

Lee had been a lifeguard here as well during the summer. My brother was so thrifty, he didn't even stay in a hotel like I did, but spent every sweaty night in an old green tent at Saint Andrew's State Park because a camping pass for the entire summer was only twenty-five dollars.

A young mother named Karen Stuart had drowned a few miles down the shore while he was a lifeguard. No one had ever since. Lee's eyes were always on the waves, even if we had been talking for twenty minutes, as if he were offering professional courtesy and assisting me in my appointed duties.

"Back then we were spaced half a mile apart from each other," he told me. "If we spotted something we'd shake a black flag and let off a airhorn." He looked down at the sand and attempted to form a mound with his foot. "They gave us walkie talkies the very next day." He pulled up on the sleeve of his shirt to reveal his farmer's tan. "Someday, someday too soon, you will even miss the color of your shoulder."

"Just go in the water," I said. "I know you want to."

He tossed his shirt underhanded to me and slipped out of his sandals. Within a minute, he was almost a hundred feet into the water, softly slapping the waves with open palms as if the ocean was an oversized and beloved pet.

While he was in the water, lost in his old memories, Dr. Fields arrived and I helped her set up her umbrella, which I now did for her every day. She gave me some green grapes as a tip.

I pointed out my brother to her and she acknowledged that fact by nodding twice, and then sat back down on her beach towel and laid on her side so she could doze off.

My brother came back in from the water and did not even notice her at first. He had the dad bod even in his early thirties, scraggly chest hair and a slight pooch above his swimsuit. Lee picked up his shirt and covered his face with it and coughed roughly.

"Would you like a can of Sunkist?" asked Dr. Fields, now lounging on her towel. She opened her cooler and pushed around some ice and picked one up. Dr. Fields held the can as if she was offering my brother an impromptu toast.

He looked at her and said thanks and took it and walked back over to me.

"Haven't seen someone drink one of these on the beach since the eighties," he said to me.

I was jealous that she had offered my brother a drink. I wanted to be the only one she was kind and generous to.

Two years ahead of him in high school, Lee remembered Dr. Fields. Her first name was Penny, she was a girl into grunge music and wore dark eyeliner and black t-shirts. He turned his gaze back to the waves and whispered to me. "You see those scars? The football coach found her one day cutting herself behind the bleachers near the field." He took a sip of soda, took a quick glance at Dr. Fields, and then looked at me. "When she was eight, nine, ten, her brother had played around with her. He had some kind of mental issue, he wasn't a Down's kid or autistic, but something was there to where he didn't go to prison or get committed." He took another sip. "She dropped out of school and got her GED, such a shame."

Back then, in those days, it was a really big deal if a girl asked out a guy on date. Celeste Rossi had asked me out just to go get frozen custard. I wasn't really attracted to her, or to anyone, at the time but I thought it was the least I could do since she had gotten up the courage. She had grown up in Panama City as well but had gone to the county high school.

We sat at a concrete table, eating vanilla custard with strawberry compote, talking about growing up. I learned that Celeste's aunt had been the young mother who had drowned.

"Were you there?" I asked.

"Yeah," she said.

"What was it like?"

"I don't know, I was a kid, I didn't really get to see anything, like you have a circle of people watching a lifeguard give mouth to mouth." It being a date, Celeste really didn't want to talk about it anymore. But she continued in a resentful tone: "All I saw was some paramedics lift a stretcher into an ambulance."

"I'm a lifeguard. I'm just curious about those things."

"Yeah. I get it. I know you're a lifeguard."

We finished our custard in silence. I awkwardly tried to change the topic. I asked her a couple of questions about majoring in music therapy and she replied with one-word answers.

That whole summer, Lee would try to schedule long weekends if he knew his wife or his daughters had plans that they couldn't cancel. The beach was especially quiet on Sunday mornings because a Presbyterian church bought an old drive-in movie theatre and refurbished into a Sunday morning venue where people could listen to a sermon in their cars while on vacation. Tourists loved the novelty of drive-in spiritual consumption.

One Sunday morning Lee told me "You've got it so good. Gosh. You won't know it for years, it may take you twenty until you can appreciate it." He then yawned, and stretched his arms behind his back then held his arms out as if surveying the ocean itself. "Work in an office on a second floor, sit in a thin chair and stare at a monitor for seven, eight hours."

"You should write lyrics for Kenny Chesney," I said.

He looked at me. "When clichés turn out to be true, that's when life jars you. That's when you realize you are an adult."

"I'm an adult," I said.

"You're fun poor. You live off microwave bean burritos and pay for gas ten bucks at a time. I'd give anything to be your age."

"Maybe the whole point about being young is not being able to appreciate it," I said. "Maybe everyone squanders their youth. Maybe we're supposed to."

My brother sat in the sand, embarrassed that he had let his thoughts be voiced. "Well, now you know why I come down so much. Trying to live vicariously off of you."

He made sure she wasn't looking then leaned over towards me in the direction of Dr. Fields. She was dozing, her book still open in her lap, as if she had fallen asleep on an airplane. "I would have fallen so hard for her if I was still a kid like you."

"Dr. Fields teaches over at Gulf Coast."

"She introduced herself as Dr. Fields?" he exclaimed. "Not Penny?"

"Yeah."

"That's gotta sting." After a moment he said. "I bet you can't even imagine what it's like to be her age."

I didn't answer, which was my way of telling him that he was right.

The day that everything happened was the last Sunday in August. A predicted high of eighty-eight degrees spoke of an unseasonably mild day. Winds were coming from the northwest, the first tease of an autumn that wouldn't truly arrive for eight more weeks. There was something wonderful about being bored on the weekdays, sitting in that white plastic chair and watching the waves slowly come in. I could let my mind wander and daydream. When there was no one swimming in my area, I felt like I was surveying my estate. Two sisters, maybe six and four, were building a sandcastle shaped like an igloo. Lee watched my area for about fifteen minutes, so I could wade into the water to get the sand off my ankles.

When I came back, he was standing next to Dr. Fields, who still lay on her towel, bragging about me, saying that I had majored in mathematics and social work. I saw her eyebrows arch in genuine surprise and then she noticed me.

"That's ambitious," she said to me as I approached them.

The oddest sound I have ever heard in my life was that of a grown man screaming from fear in a squeaky voice. The man was carrying an unconscious boy as he stomped through the water, which was up to his knees. He had almost reached the sand when his foot landed poorly and he fell face first into the water while still managing to hold onto the boy.

I heard my brother's voice behind me as I ran towards them. "Hang on, we're lifeguards."

"It's going to be okay," I yelled. "Let me have him."

By the time I reached them, the father had gotten back to his knees, still holding the boy, who looked to be about eight. His skin had not yet turned blue.

"Let me have him," I repeated.

The father laid him in my arms and I put him down right on the edge of the wet sand.

"I'll go get the kit," said Lee, fear in his own voice. "Don't do anything, wait for me to come back."

The boy's yellow hair was cropped close. Strangely in that moment I thought to myself that his mother should let his hair grow out.

I put my face next to his, no air out of his tiny nostrils, no air out of his mouth. I laid my head over his heart to listen but I couldn't hear anything. My efforts at cpr seemed mechanical.

"Come on Caleb, you're okay buddy, you're okay, you're going to be okay," said his father.

Lee came back, angry. "Your kit only had rubbing alcohol and aloe vera, how could you be so stupid," He barked. I had forgotten his strength for he pushed me away with both hands.

His efforts did not revive the boy.

"Ya'll are the lifeguards, save him!" The father screamed. After a moment he whimpered, "Oh please save him."

The boy's face began to turn slightly less red.

People on the beach began to realize what was happening and started to gather around us in a circle like they did in tv and movies.

One of those people was Dr. Fields, who pushed my brother away from the boy. Without saying a word, she lifted the boy's rigid body up and laid him across her lap. I swear to you that the first thing I thought of was Michelangelo's Pietà from my art history class. All of the adversities she had endured in her life, being sexually abused, cutting herself, having the whole school find out, and then having to move back to her hometown where everyone still remembered, those were burdens she had borne, yet, or perhaps because of them, she had the strength to sift through her emotions and calmly help a boy on the beach. She put her pointer and middle finger together and jabbed the boy's throat underneath his Adam's apple.

Gasp, air, cough, gasp, air, the boy coughed up dark pieces of beef jerky that were lodged in his throat and had obstructed his breathing. The boy had not been drowning and his father had been too panicked to remember to tell them that it was food, not water that caused the lack of oxygen.

Dr. Fields sat him up and wiped the meat down onto his chest and then swept it onto the sand.

I glanced at my brother. Lee looked as stunned as I was.

The father let Dr. Fields continue to hold his son but he hugged both of them together.

The boy asked for water and then coughed dryly. "Can I have some water?" he asked a second time. But there were no bottles of water around and the fountain by the bathrooms was almost a hundred yards away.

Dr. Fields stood up and then stood up the boy and walked back to her chair and took the can of Sunkist that was in the chair's cup holder and gave it to the boy to drink, which he did with both hands and then we all heard the sirens of an arriving ambulance.

That night my brother and I had a miserable meal at a Waffle House. We were two fools that had talked like we were princes of the sand, knights in shining armor willing to save anyone, anytime. Neither of us felt like talking, we were shamed into silence and he drove home afterwards. I took melatonin to try to get sleepy but the sleepy sensation left as quickly as it had arrived. I stayed up all night and walked to a playground and sat in a swing, laying my head against the chain. It was so humid, it felt like I was taking a shower. Any breeze that came brought heat, not relief. Exhausted, I fell asleep in the swing as the night sky was turning navy blue indicating the arrival of an approaching dawn. The next day I was let go, but I would have quit otherwise.

Back then everyone had their home address listed in the phone book, which is how I found Dr. Field's address. Later that night I walked to a nearby snack bar where I bought a cherry slushy and a grape slushy then I got in my car and headed towards a cloudless sunset and the North Bay bridge near to where she lived about six miles away.

The breeze wasn't the same in this part of town. It felt less feral, less wild, more bland and suburban than the sandy winds I felt in my white chair on the beach. I parked my car and then with a slushy in each hand I approached her place and realized that she did not live in a house, like I thought all adults over thirty did, but in an orange and brown brick four unit apartment building with a decorative black stairwell that was gaudy at best.

There were four slots for mail by the stairwell and I saw that her name listed on the C unit slot so I walked up the steps and took a deep breath and then put down the drinks and knocked. I felt like such a little kid, asking myself why did I buy her a slushy instead of bringing her some flowers?

After a moment, I heard someone moving to the door and when she opened it I realized that the whole summer I had been in love with her. She was wearing a faded black shirt and ripped denim shorts and holding a remote control in her hand.

"Hello Pete," she said.

"Hi, I, I brought you a slushy as a thank you." Blushing, I could barley look her in the face. "I have cherry and I have grape. I know it's stupid; I should have gotten you orange because I know you love Sunkist—"

"Grape sounds wonderful," she interrupted. Dr. Fields did not invite me into her apartment, but instead walked out to the little walkway past me.

I followed her as she walked to the back of the second floor stoop and then handed her the slushy. You could see the bridge, and the sun, one third of it having already gone. It was not a view of emerald-colored Caribbean water, but it was still a view of water. People from Indiana and Oklahoma and Kentucky drove fourteen hours in cramped cars and dirty minivans just to see this water, whitish-brown from the sand of north Florida.

After she took a long sip, she said "I rented this apartment for the view."

"It's nice," I said.

She didn't reply.

"I'm so happy that you saved him. It was my job to save his life and I couldn't. That boy would have died if you hadn't been there."

She took another sip of her drink. "I took a Red Cross certification class a few summers ago because I was bored."

"I should have gotten you flowers or something more than a stupid slushy." I was tired, I realized, and then I felt myself crying. I threw my drink off the porch into the street below. And then I wiped my eyes.

She handed me her drink. "You can throw this one as well if it will make you feel better."

"Thanks," I said. And I did.

Dr. Fields gathered me into her chest and held me. Her perfume smelled like wet flowers. Her fingernails gently scratched my scalp and I never wanted that moment to end. I don't know how much time passed, I just remember her backing up and putting a hand on each of my shoulders, tilting her head slightly down and looking directly at me with her green eyes. "People save each other's lives everyday. Sometimes they don't even know that they do."

We looked at each other.

"Who saved your life?" I asked.

"What do you mean?"

"Who got you to quit cutting yourself?"

She took her hands off my shoulders and looked at me with a trace of anger. I had asked a question that she did not want to answer.

"No one has," she finally said. Taking a step back from me, Dr. Fields pulled her shorts up until they shaped a bikini. There were other cuts that looked newer. "Old habits are hard to break. I go to the beach to tan them away."

Neither of us said anything for a moment.

"I could be that person," I said.

"How would you save me Pete?" she asked.

I looked down at my sandy feet and black sandals. "I don't know but I'd like to try."

The trace of anger seemed to evaporate on her face and her eyes softened. "Have a good night Pete," she said and then went back inside her apartment and closed the door.

The sun would not completely set until almost nine that evening. I sat in my car with the engine running and the windows down, wondering if I should go back to her apartment. I never got to call her Penny or put my palms on her face and kiss her. Perhaps to her, I was an overgrown boy with puppy love, dopesick with infatuation, and she was too weary and sober-eyed. A few days later I knocked on her door, but she was not there or maybe she simply did not answer the door.

Now I am older than Dr. Fields was then. I left the beach life soon after and became an actuary with a wife and two sons and a mortgage on a split-level house six hours from the beach. Now when I return to Panama City Beach on vacation I sit on the white sands and watch my family make a sandcastle without me. I tell my wife it's the lifeguard in me, I just need to view the scene: the sand, the water, and the people walking by.

Secretly, I hope that one day I will see a woman walk nearby and plant an umbrella, spread out a beach blanket, and then take a can of Sunkist out of a small red cooler. I know it will be her because she will be the last person in America that still drinks Sunkist. Then Dr. Fields will recognize me and shake her head as if I was an old flame. She will hold up her orange can of soda and silently offer it to me, and I would walk to her and take the drink. Popping the top, the carbonation would cause the foamy soda to bubble over onto my hand and I would down the ice-cold syrupy beverage so quickly that it would cause my gums to hurt. And that is as close as I will ever hope to describe what love is.

Dick Cheney Shot Me in the Face
by Timothy O'Leary

I was crouched half-mast, watching my bird dog Belle nudge a sharp-tail out of a patch of tubey buffalo grass, when Dick Cheney shot me in the face. If you know anything about shotguns, the fact I'm alive to tell this story borders on a miracle. Lucky for me the Vice-President was shooting small—an ancient 20-gauge packed with bird shot, supposedly a gun Gerald Ford gave Dick in 1974 for running his Presidential campaign.

Jesus, if I have to hear that story one more time.

If he'd been using a grownup's gun, a 12 or 16-gauge, it would've been closed-coffin. At the very least I'd be sucking dinner through a straw while watching cartoons from a chrome wheelchair. Fortunate the Vice-President couldn't hit a barn door from thirty feet. He favors himself quite the sportsman, but after hunting and fishing with the guy for thirty years I can tell you there's a lot of *legend* in Cheneyville. Fact is, Dick rattles easy. A real jumpy guy. When those wings whistle and a grouse goes vertical he does a little Halliburton two-step, all excited like he just got to invade another Arab country. A man who understands hunting plants himself, calmly leading the bird.

Ironically, his shitty hunting skills saved my life. I only took the tail-end of the load, though to this day I've no clue what he was shooting at. What I can say is that getting shot in the face is a life changing experience. I'd turned my head a touch when I heard the blast, and next thing I know I'm lifted off my feet and tipped over, pellets burrowing a quarter inch into my face and neck like big iron ticks.

The scalp is a big bleeder, and when there's that much blood you can't tell how hurt you are. I mean, nick your leg with a chainsaw and you can at least see if it's still attached. But good luck figuring out a head wound. I lay there, wondering if this was it, one eye, blind with blood, the one I lost that day. Through the other I could see him bent at the waist, staring down on me, even whiter than normal. Corpse white, that artificial ticker maybe not pumping all the way to his brain. The sun at his back, his sweaty bald head and glasses reflecting light, there was this eerie halo around him, like some kind of warped angel. I thought, "If I'm dead and Cheney's here, something's gone terribly, terribly wrong."

"Henry? For God's sake Henry, are you alright?"

And that was the last time I ever saw Dick Cheney.

Next thing I know he's whisked away by a couple Secret Service guys, Lurch and Larry I liked to call them. You'd have thought it was Dick that'd been shot, men yelling into their sleeves, "Angler out, Angler out." Angler, his code name. Jesus, we don't have anglers in the West, we have fishermen. But Dick has to be all Isaac Walton, or act like a British lord making a big ta-do. Cheney, man of the land, slayer of fish. Hell, when he casts a fly it's more apt to end up in the back of someone's head than a rainbow's mouth. If Dick's in the boat, de-barb those hooks and duck for cover!

Big black Escalades tore through my field, and like magic men surrounded Dick, shoving him like a sleeping bag head-first into the back. And me? I'm left lying in the dirt, blood piddling down my face, Belle whimpering as she circled me. I reached up to feel the lead pellets lodged in my skull before holding out a limp hand to comfort her, Belle sniffing hard to see if she smelled death.

Finally, a couple more of the big boys hoisted me up and laid me flat in the back of a four-wheeler, me yelling, "Don't forget Belle," and off we went, bouncing up and down on hard carpet, tearing up even more of my wheat. I smelled iron, unsure if it's blood or just the normal odor of a government rig; the pungent bouquet of bullshit. Once we hit the highway they lit up the siren and it's off to the hospital in Jackson Hole, shock and awe all the way, everything around pulling to the side, this being one instance when I appreciated executive power.

For the next hour they tweezed pellets out of my noggin and neck. Cleaned out my eye socket to someday fit me with a glass peeper. When I awoke, my wife Cindy was bedside, angry and worried, rocking in her seat, fists balled as if she's preparing to mount a horse that don't particularly want to be ridden.

"I told you not to go. Man's a menace. But no, you're a big shot. Hunting with the Vice President. Big goddamn deal. See what that gets you? Your head near blown off, and damn near blind."

Cindy-speak for, "Oh my God, how are you feeling?" And me thinking it's a good thing Dick didn't kill me, because the next image in my mind is Cindy beating Cheney to death with that leather-strapped sawed-off pool cue she keeps under the front car seat. "Just in case I run into someone lacking manners," is how she explains the weapon.

A few minutes later some other pencil-neck crept into my room. I'd seen him a couple times hovering around Dick. Pure Washington, but "westernized" in a leather vest and shiny black shit-kickers.

"Mr. Thomas," he said, and shakes his head with fake concern. "I'm Lawrence Hovey. I work for the Vice President. How are you? I'm so happy to see you awake and looking so good under the circumstances." He smiled like a man who just farted and plans to blame the dog.

I eyed him, with what was left of me, and grunted. "Where's Dick?"

"The Vice President was called back to Washington. An emergency. But he wanted me to check in on you, make sure you're comfortable and have everything you need. We did some background on the surgeon here, a real top-notch fellow, as good as you could get anywhere in the country."

I didn't mention what little comfort that was for a man with an empty crater in his head. Instead, I pondered myself with an eye patch, like Lee Marvin in Cat Ballou.

"So, Mr. Thomas, as you can imagine this is a pretty sensitive situation. The press and all. If they get wind of a hunting accident they'll have a field day. The Vice President has to deal with them on a daily basis. The personal intrusions, the insults, all part of his job. But you certainly didn't sign up for that, did you? It's important we have a discussion on the best way to handle this. You know, to protect you and your family. The press can be very disruptive."

Cindy poked at him with her long index finger, the "finger of truth" I call it, and with the power to cut through bullshit. "Disruptive?" she yelled. "Know what's disruptive? Being blind. Walking around with a white cane and a dog to lead you to the bathroom. Making your living with a tin cup and a dancing monkey as your partner. That's disruptive."

I appreciated Cindy's flair for drama, but clearly I was only half blind and didn't require any assistance from an animal. Turning towards Hovey I said, "You don't need to worry. I'm not talking to the press," which sounded like "Snu dan't ned to voory," my lips still rubbery from the anesthesia.

Fact is, if I wanted to tell tales about Dick Cheney, I'd have a lot more to talk about than his lack of field-sport skills. Dick and I, we'd been acquainted most of my life. We met at Natrona High School in Casper in the 50's. I wouldn't say we were friends, but we shared a love of beer, which sometimes brings men together. After we graduated the government offered me a vacation abroad, all expenses paid, as in "C'mon kid, see the world, beginning with Vietnam." And Dick, well, he had a real aversion to uniforms, racked up five deferments, and became one of the most legendary draft dodgers in Wyoming history.

I went off to Texas for boot camp then shipped overseas, first time I'd ever been outside of Wyoming. I didn't follow politics much; at that age it was all ice-cold brew and girls. I just knew my Dad and Granddad had served their time in the big wars, and if the country needed me it was my duty to show up. Most of us in Wyoming felt that way, which is why I couldn't figure Dick out.

The Army tended to regard country boys as pack mules, finding us jobs we'd be doing at home, primarily walking across fields shooting at stuff. But in Vietnam stuff tended to shoot back, which kind of changed the whole experience. There were a lot of adjustments. In Wyoming it sometimes might hit 100 degrees, but never with 100% humidity, and you don't have seven-foot long snakes that can swallow a good-sized dog. Or little kids that will accept a Hershey or Mounds bar with one hand and shoot your nuts off with the other.

I did, however, learn a few useful skills. I can now rig a bicycle seat with a tiny bit of C4 so it blows your ass thirty feet skyward. I got real good at stuffing a grenade down a rabbit hole while running full-tilt. My marksmanship improved. I can pretty much plant one dead center in the brain bucket from two hundred yards. Or at least I could until Cheney shot out my sighting eye.

Of course, I'm no longer defending the war. When I got out and took the time to educate myself about the political hi-jinx and economic motivations, I developed a different perspective. I'm still proud of those of us who did the job. The army—the working grunts—ain't about politics. It's about getting done what needs to be done, following orders, and if you're lucky, surviving.

But Cheney managed to avoid the good and bad of that life experience. Instead of boot camp he opted for Yale, where he promptly flunked out. Twice. Don't get me wrong. Cheney never struck me so much as a dumb man as he did the overly-confident sort, a guy with an amazingly high opinion of himself. My guess is that he just thought he knew better than all those professors.

I ran into him when I was home on leave, Dick spending his time trying to talk yet another college into keeping him out of harm's way. We ended up hoisting a few, Dick real curious about military life, and full of questions about Nam. He's decided it was about the last place he wanted to be, and if the military came breathing down his neck he'd join the Coast Guard.

"The Coast Guard? Dick, you've never been near a body of water you couldn't swim across while holding a can of Bud. What the hell do you know about boats and the ocean?"

"All I need to know is that any coast I'd be guarding would be seven thousand miles from Vietnam. Hell, maybe they'll put me down south protecting Malibu Beach. Keep watch over all those girls in bikinis. The kind of duty I might enjoy." Dick has a way of saying things, no matter how stupid, with such confidence that you almost want to believe him.

We were in his Dad's pickup, three sheets to the wind, headed to our fourth watering hole when Dick drove into a ditch, taking out twenty feet of fence and awarding him the first of his two DUIs. Me? I ended up in the hospital, ten stitches in my forehead. It occurs to me now that the scars on my face are a map of Cheney's screw-ups.

I lost track of him for quite a few years, and next thing I heard he's a big shot in Washington, working first for some Congressman, and then as an assistant to President Ford. Pretty amazing to everyone who knew him back home. We all figured it must not be all that tough to become a success in Washington.

After my honorable discharge I married Cindy, who'd always been the one and only for me, and we worked my dad's spread until he died. Then we sold his tired place, moved to Jackson Hole, and managed to buy a lot of land in the valley when it was just another nothing Wyoming town. Twenty years later the Richie Riches start moving in from everywhere, building fake multi-million dollar ranches and hunting lodges, a lot of them oil men that would visit now and then to see their money bubble out of the ground. Followed by the Hollywood-types. They could hide on a thousand acres, still find a good steak, and there was no income tax. "C'mon out to the ranch and we'll go fly fishing or go skiing," they'd say to their fancy friends.

During tourist season the streets filled with "cityidiots" buying two hundred dollar Stetsons, and silver-tipped Tony Llamas. And suddenly I'm selling ground to these knuckleheads for fifty, even a hundred times what I paid for it, and I wake up one day an average guy with a good bit of coin. Until then our biggest dream had been to make the bank payments, and maybe have enough left over to drive to Denver every couple years to see the Broncos play, this "rich" thing a total surprise.

Which is about the time I hooked up again with Cheney. He was running for Congress, comes to town for a fundraiser, and of course hits me up for a donation. Then Dick wants to shoot birds or an elk, maybe bring some of his big donors out to "his good friend Henry's" spread to catch some cutthroat. Make him appear a man of the land. A real American.

Okay, Cindy doesn't lie. I fell for it. I was pretend friends with Cheney. Me. Mr. Big Shot. I admit I loved going into town and have the boys ask, "How's your buddy the Congressman?" I'm not the kind of guy would ever ask for anything, but somehow it made me feel important just knowing I could. Not proud of that, but it's a fact.

To make it worse, Cheney kept working his way through Washington like a nasty strain of flu. Next thing you know he's Secretary of Defense. Right, the guy who avoided the Army like a grungy toilet seat. The way I see it, if you're put in charge of sending men to war, you ought to damn well have been there yourself, seen firsthand what human carnage looks like up close. Taking in a Rambo flick won't do.

After that he's a Bush fixture, so we weren't surprised when he got named Vice President under Junior. Once a year or so I'd get the call: "Vice President Cheney is scheduled in Jackson and he'd like to come out to your place," more an order than a request.

It had nothing to do with friendship. We never engaged in heartfelt discussions, just two guys getting older discussing all they had learned. No deep thinking from Dick, who tended to focus on his own paranoia, infused with a lot of hate. Cheney was like a turn-of-the–century aristocrat, Baron Baldy Von Uptight, he and his old white men cronies, living in the old days while the rest of the world moved on. Though we were waving the same flag, Dick's America sure looked a lot different than mine.

But I wasn't about to tell *that* story, that we were really just using each other. I have no desire to be seen wearing an eye patch in People Magazine or sitting across from Larry King. OK, I might like to sit with that Katie Couric. She's got some firecracker in her. But no interest in the press. Not my style.

In other words, I never said a thing.

And guess who else never said a thing, Dick Cheney. You might've thought he'd call and apologize. Send over a nice bottle of scotch with a card, "Sorry I can't shoot straight, keep an eye out for me." Hell, I'd of laughed over that.

About a year later I saw he did it again. Apparently too embarrassed to hunt in Wyoming, Dick travelled to Texas and shot someone else in the face. Naturally, I'm interested. Dick's hunting with an old fellow named Harry Whittington, and it's pretty much a repeat performance, only way rougher for Harry. He's also hit in the chest, and while he's in the hospital has a heart attack and a lung collapses. Harry took a bigger load, around 200 pellets, and to this day some of the metal is still inside him, too close to vitals to yank out. Your body has a way of cleaning itself up, sometimes working shrapnel to the surface. I think about poor Harry, sitting at breakfast, when he feels a BB bubble-up, a bloody little thing popping out of his chest while he sips his coffee, just to remind him of Dick.

The sad thing? Harry barely knew Cheney. He'd donated a few bucks, was asked to go hunting, and next thing he's in the hospital and they're putting paddles to him. Then the press converges, hounding him for weeks. Cheney's people made a half-assed attempt to blame Harry, as if he'd jumped in front of a man firing a shotgun. But from what I could tell Harry's a straight shooter, not saying much, not blaming anyone. Just acting the southern gentleman. But one thing that particularly caught my attention. When the press asked him if Dick ever apologized, Harry smiled and changed the subject.

And I couldn't help but feel guilty. If I'd come forward when Dick shot me, maybe Harry would've thought twice about going hunting with the guy. The idea haunted me, until I just decided we had to talk, one Cheney survivor to another. So I call down to his law office in Austin. It's tough to get through. I'm sure he's tired of people bringing up the subject, so I leave him a voice mail. A couple days later he calls back, and I can tell he's skeptical, but we talk, and after a while get comfortable, discovering we've got more in common than the fact Dick Cheney shot us. Harry seemed the kind of man I'd appreciate sitting down and having a drink with, his head screwed on straight. Certainly a conservative type, but we share the belief that America also stands for a level playing field. It didn't devolve into a Cheney bitch session, but it did occur to us that hanging around with him was dangerous to our health, and maybe dangerous for other reasons too. When you stand behind a man people naturally assume you also stand for him, and I suspect we both saw a different kind of America than Dick.

We discussed living on the land, driving down dirt roads, thinking what a wonder that God put us in such a place. And here's what you learn when you live in the country: Part of being a good neighbor is warning people about dangerous situations, and yes, keeping an eye out for each other. When I'm driving and come across a herd of elk crossing the road, or see a patch of black ice, I flash my lights to warn oncoming cars. When my neighbors are safe, I'm safe.

The Stones of Sorrow Lake
by Brenda Peynado

I pressed my face to the car window to see Jackson's hometown, the place we'd spent all our money moving to after graduation, the place we would be stuck in. It was June, the month of green. Willows everywhere wept over houses and cars and one little girl riding her bicycle. Wind from the lake fanned over waving cornfields, and when the road got close to the waterfront, the lake shone brightly over the town. Instead of sand, the shore was made of smooth stones, both large and small. Townspeople stood at the shore, some with arms outstretched, staring into the waves, and others kneeling with palms open, as if to catch something falling from the sky.

"That," said Jackson, "is our lake of sorrow."

*

Jackson often flashed the pockmark scar on his arm, but I didn't know what sorrow was behind it. He said he was too young to remember. The scars and the stones—they happened to nearly everyone in the town.

When the townspeople encountered their first great grief—not something small like a broken leg or a bickering between friends, but real grief, the kind that brought you to

194

your knees—the first time they felt that, their stone of sorrow would form. Sometimes it happened when they were still children: a father who left, a great divorce, a twin who died. Sometimes it happened when they were teens. A few were lucky enough to escape it until they were older, or had somehow steeled themselves against it.

But whenever they felt that sorrow, that's when the rock started forming—in their fists, in their praying palms, in their throats. At first it was as small as a grain of sand they couldn't wash away, irritating. Then it would roll into a pebble over a matter of minutes or years. Sometimes it only grew as big as a skipping stone, sometimes as big as a boulder. Everyone's sorrow took its own course and speed, and no amount of forced catharsis or letting go could make the rock go away when you wanted. In its own time the stone would dislodge, but only when it could fall on the shore of the lake. You could see the townspeople at the shore every dawn and sunset, orange light on their faces, hoping their rocks would dislodge, would lie down with their comrades of sorrow, generations of them along the water line.

You knew which rock was yours. It called to you if you went too far away, and some of the townspeople carved their names on theirs. The townspeople were tied to that lake—which is why so few of them ever were able to leave town for any long period of time, if at all. Even Jackson could feel it calling to him, which is why he'd wanted to move back to his hometown when we graduated—but only temporarily, just until we saved up, had better luck, could find jobs in the city and move downstate.

He'd wanted to move here alone. He said he was embarrassed to be moving back with his parents, and we could be long-distance for a while. But something about that story didn't sit right with me. I thought it must have been his sorrow calling to him—the lake, his stone he said he was too young to remember. So, I told him I was coming with him and kept at it until he gave in.

The way he talked about his home was so different from my own family stories from the Dominican Republic. I kept imagining the snow and ice of upstate winters and peering into these stories Jackson told, as if I were peering into a snow globe. You could shake it and down fell that white glitter with the promise it would keep swirling and swirling around those tragic, trapped figures, and if you stared too long you might find yourself inside it. And here I was, moving there, expecting to hate it. I wanted Jackson to tell stories about me instead, about our first summer in town, about the kids we would have and the tragedies we would hold each other through.

*

After the twenty-hour drive, we were ready to uncurl, shower, sleep. But when we rolled close to his parents' house, Jackson said, "Oh no."

Streamers were strung across trees in the driveway, and a giant sign said WELCOME HOME. The whole town had turned out, milling over Jackson's parents' land. There were kids playing with toys, dogs running about, people heaping food on paper plates by the picnic bench. A woman I recognized from the pictures as Jackson's mother waved her hands at us from the porch and called everyone to attention while we parked.

I took a deep breath and got out of the car.

"Surprise!" they yelled. "Welcome home!"

Jackson's father shook my hand. "We didn't think you would come."

"Ed..." Jackson's mother said. "He means we thought you'd never get here."

"Surprise," I said.

The town whirled around me, clutching my hand and saying "Finally," and "Welcome," and "Nice to meet you." They clapped me on the back, introducing themselves in a mad rush. A few of them had stones on their shoulders like parakeets. One girl shook my hand and the stone in her palm felt smooth and cool. Many of the rest had visible scars. The children, for the most part, ran around un-marred, unburdened.

It was the kind of small town where everyone's sorrow was memorized in a litany. Jackson had told me their sto-ries. Their families had lived there a hundred years or more, off the land and the lake, planting in the summer, ice fish-ing and hiding from the lake-effect snow in the winter. Most of Jackson's friends were drug addicts or ex-drug ad-dicts—your options when you can't get away from a place and you can feel the stones on the shore calling. Three guys hugged me with trembling arms or pinpricked-pupil eyes.

These were the kind of people I had been taught to look down on, theirs the sorrows I was meant to pity. You could tell they thought the same about me, poor me, without sor-row. But I'd felt pain before. There was nothing about this one town that made them holier than the rest, just because they wore their scars on their skin. Still, I laughed and smiled, because what could you do in the face of all those visible sorrows?

There was Jackson's high school best friend, called Panda because he looked giant and cuddly, but I knew that Panda had killed someone in a fight the next town over while he was still in school. That had been his sorrow, even though the other boy had started it. And even though the fight was years ago, Panda still hadn't lost his stone, which grew between his shoulder blades—a boulder that made him hunch and unable to sit in chairs. He worked construction, but that boulder made it almost impossible. He needed the money, though. He had been putting up bricks on the top story of a house while he was on painkillers and lost his balance. The boulder tipped him right over. He fell two stories straight down on his back and survived, but the story he was telling now was about how he was suing the construction company for an unsafe workspace. He was winning the suit, too. I heard him say to someone in the crowd, "Oh, my back, my back." To someone else he said, "We're about to be millionaires."

As he went to give me a hug, Panda said, winking, "So you're the new squeeze," and kissed me on the cheek the way he must have heard my people do it.

"Have you heard about June?" he said to Jackson.

Jackson put his arm around my shoulder. His lips were pressed thin and he squeezed me tight. "Best month to see upstate for the first time, isn't it?"

Panda had married a woman named Barbie with one jagged scar down her check where a stone had grown and fallen off within one day, so big when it appeared that they had to carry her to the lake where she laid kneeling, cheek to the shore. With her, it's that she got married to her first husband at seventeen, and then he had died in a car crash, just slipped off the ice on a road cutting over a cliff. She was supposed to go out with him that night but she had been feeling sick. Panda was her third husband. The second one she'd married at nineteen, and he died by drowning. It didn't matter how many sorrows you had—only the first one grew a stone, made physical the memory that would keep calling you back to those shores your whole life.

Barbie tried to keep everyone away from Panda because she was convinced he would divorce her before the millions came through. When he handed me a beer, she shuttled him away toward the picnic tables, her scar caving into a grimace.

I touched my cheek.

"Don't worry," Jackson said. "We're not staying long enough for you to get one of those, just to save up some. We'll be out of here before you know it. In the city before you can blink."

He pointed out others from the town; the mayor, his high-school basketball coach, his two sisters, his brother's new baby who had Down Syndrome. The shy sister, now a fifth-grade teacher at the one elementary school, barely spoke to me as she sat her beautiful two boys at the picnic table with cut-up chicken and melting Popsicles.

One of the sister's knees was swollen, and she had the leg sticking out away from the picnic bench so I had to step over. She had a tumor in there that had spread, and they couldn't operate. At first, when everyone had seen the growing, they thought it was a stone, a second one under the scar of the stone she'd dropped. But they all knew that wasn't how it worked and eventually they figured out it was cancer—which explained the stones clinging to the foreheads of her two little boys, who must have known by now how serious things were for their mother. The boys played whiffle ball beside us. I said hi to the boys, told them how great I thought their whiffle ball form was, but they grimaced their distaste for me on their Popsicle-smeared faces.

Jackson whispered, "They do that to everyone but their mother. You'll get along fine here."

But why wasn't I sure? The night before, we had fallen asleep on a pallet of blankets on the empty apartment floor. We had held hands over our heads, we had run fingertips over the lines of our palms. I loved him—his scar, how his smile always ringed his eyes with lines, how he was the stronger of the two of us, how he was the one who could pull himself away from the sorrow on these shores calling to him. Even though he had had to come back, eventually. I didn't think I could be that strong. On the long drive we had only fought once, because of me making goofy animal noises to a song and giggling, a laughter that somehow had grated on him. "I'm just being silly," I said, but then he asked me to drive for a few hours.

In line by the bowls and heaps of food, Jackson introduced me to his friend Samantha. I knew there was a stone inside her mouth, big enough she couldn't speak around it. It glinted gray between the lines of her teeth when she smiled. With her it was that her brother, the valedictorian, the one they thought was going to get out but couldn't pry himself away from his first sorrow, killed himself in the back room of the one pizza shop in town where he had worked. The pizza shop closed soon after, bankrupting that family, which turned out to be someone else's sorrow. Samantha handed me a paper plate, pointed at my Mana T-shirt, and moved her hips around a little as if she wished she could dance merengue. I was relieved that she didn't ask me questions and I didn't have to make conversation. I could feel myself relaxing a little, breathing for the first time since we arrived.

Every time someone would look at us, Jackson held my hand underneath the picnic table. I looked around the party at the people clumped together in their groups, and Jackson and I stuck with the children now that everyone had said hello. I kept hearing people whispering the word *June* all around me, and I'd never seen a month so beautiful and new. The air still smelled slightly of chicken shit, but then the wind would pour through the trees surrounding the clearing and I'd catch wafts of jasmine and lavender, or something that smelled like them. The sky was blue and clear like an ocean I could walk into and float on. Spiders and ants ran on the table, and big fuzzy bees landed in the children's hair. If this was what Jackson was called back to, the June in his memory, I could dream it with him. I saw him as a little boy with the same tight-lipped smile, skipping other people's sorrows across the lake.

*

"Let's talk to Gramps," Jackson said when we were done eating, and we threw our plates away and stepped over the extension cord juicing the refrigerator on the porch. I knew Jackson's father had built the porch the summer after he'd been accepted to the FBI. Of course, he'd never left the day he was supposed to go to Quantico; Jackson had told me he was too afraid of straying from the shore of the lake. For Jackson's father it was that boys from out of town held him down and made him watch them rape his girlfriend, Jackson's mother. Jackson's mother already had a stone growing over one of her eyes from a previous sorrow, so she just closed her eyes until they were done. They never found the boys, never knew who they were. So he couldn't leave to Quantico, of course he couldn't.

Jackson's grandpa and the old men stood near the beer fridge comparing stories, the creaky porch shifting with their weight. By the look of it, they'd heard them all before. Most of the men had large scars on their forearms or biceps, and they spent much of their time drinking at the VA in the center of town. His grandpa still hadn't lost his stone—he kept refusing to go to the lake all these years to let it drop. The stone bulged from his stomach like a beer belly under his shirt. Jackson hugged his grandpa around that belly, challenged him to a game of ping-pong he knew he would lose.

"I'll do you one better," his grandpa said. "Why don't we take this little lady off your hands?"

"But can I trust you not to get her drunk?" Jackson said.

"Sure," said one of them, winking.

Cups appeared from the vets' pockets, the telescoping metal kind that come with flasks, and a small table was unfolded in the center of the porch. One of them patted on a camping chair and pointed at me to sit down. Jackson stepped back a few feet. We made a circle with the cups in front of us, all of them filled, somebody said, with moonshine from someone's barn.

"What are the rules to the game?" I asked.

The vets harrumphed, and Jackson stepped back close to me.

"It's not a game," he whispered, "Just listen."

"Just leave her with us," Jackson's grandfather told him. "We'll take care of her."

Panda was waving Jackson over to another corner of the yard.

"I'll be fine," I said.

"I'll be right back," Jackson promised, walking down the porch stairs.

His grandpa began talking: "I fell in love when I was sixteen with a girl who could speak to animals. Fifty years of happiness with goats, squirrels, deer living in the house. Then she died. That was worse than war. I was lucky in that my sorrow didn't come until I was old. I didn't even stay in this danged town because of sorrow. It was for love. I stayed for her and because she had a sorrow—her best friend, her dog, dying in her arms. Then I get stuck here as soon as she quits this place."

He patted his stomach, the stone there.

Another vet said, almost in a chant, "What is love but an eventual sorrow? What is love but a stone waiting to happen?"

Everyone took a drink and I followed cue. Dust caked everything I touched. Our first shot, I swallowed whiskey-floating balls of dust.

The vet to his left, with so many pocked scars across his arms and face, said, "When I went to Nam, I had a baby with a girl from Da Nang. Then a friend stepped on a landmine and I got peppered by shrapnel. They sent me home. The fall of Saigon happened while I was out of it. Been looking for her ever since."

He touched one particular scar on his forearm that he'd tattooed over with the insignia of his company. Everyone drank. You could hear the kids laughing and yelling just beyond the porch bannisters. Samantha came onto the porch and sat down on the floor next to me. They pulled out another metal cup, and when she drank from it you could hear it clink against the stone in her mouth.

The third vet, his bottom teeth missing and his lips curled round the gums, started. He said his older sister, the one who let him sleep in her bed when he was frightened, had died from pneumonia when he was ten. Another said his best friend died in his arms from a gunshot. He'd had to be given an honorable discharge because his stone had grown into his skin, into his brain; after this vet's homecoming, townspeople had to carry him to the lake. His skull was still soft in that spot.

Another said he'd tried to start a feed store before he went to Nam. It had taken all his savings, bankrupted him when the store from the next town over got all the business. He didn't even get drafted; he'd enlisted out of shame. Another's best friend had embezzled everything they had. He was the same vet who chanted earlier. He added, "What's a friend but the one who will eventually betray you?"

Panda lumbered up the porch, his arm around Barbie, who shouldered some of the burden of his weight. "Can I join?" he asked. He sat on the floor where the stone on his back wouldn't get in the way.

Samantha was next, and then me. I thought surely they'd know I didn't have a stone. Samantha couldn't say anything. She just tilted her head back, opened her mouth wide. She hummed with her mouth open like that, a gray song. We drank.

"What about you?" Jackson's grandfather asked me.

I was already pretty tipsy. I was sure, so sure, that I had my own pain, too. But after hearing all they'd suffered, how could I, without wearing a rock or a scar to prove it? No great loves before Jackson. My parents and friends were all still alive. The relatives who had died were across the ocean, and I had barely known them. In that moment, drunk as I was, the only thing I could remember that hit me the hardest was how my face fell when Jackson turned away from me if I horsed around, like somehow my lightness was an insult. But that wasn't a sorrow. That was such a small thing.

"Don't think I have one," I said. "Not yet."

They exchanged looks, and I was sure they were thinking, *One of those.*

Barbie sniffed, crossing her arms.

The circle kept going, and now and then Jackson beamed his smile from across the yard. Once, I saw what I thought was a young girl throwing a ball at his face, but then I realized the ball in her palm was actually a stone and would not dislodge. Eventually Jackson walked towards the porch to check on me.

Barbie saw him coming. "Hey Jackson!" she said. "Come join in. Give us yours."

He shrugged. "That's okay," he said, glancing at me.

"He doesn't remember it," I said, pretty drunk and glad there was something I could talk about as if I knew the answer.

Everyone looked at me, brows furrowed. Samantha started humming again. Jackson put his hands in his pockets and started back down the stairs.

"Come on," Panda called to him, "June's getting married."

"Forget it," Jackson yelled back.

June, the month of bees and welcome. June, a girl I imagined clad with weeping willow branches, her eyes like honey, who always took everything seriously. I was too drunk to stand up and pick my way around Jackson's grandfather where he was blocking the stairs to the porch. "Gramps," I said, "I need to go."

"Go ahead," he said, "hit me in the stomach. I promise it won't hurt."

Panda punched him, and Jackson's grandfather fell down from his chair. I think I gasped, and then he stood back up, laughing at his prank. "Told ya it wouldn't hurt," he said.

Everyone was grinning, but I could see they were sad for me, suddenly. They were the kind of people who could laugh as they cried.

*

I stumbled across the lawn to where Jackson was tossing a Frisbee for one of the dogs. "Who's June?" I said. "Why is everyone mentioning her?"

Jackson looked down at the dog while he yanked the Frisbee out of its mouth.

"Who is she?" I asked again.

Finally he said, "It was so long ago…"

"Okay. I'm listening."

"June," he said, squinting into the sun, "was my first sorrow."

"I thought you didn't remember it." I let out my breath, fell backwards into the grass and lay there.

"It doesn't mean anything," he said. He stood over me, blocking the sun. He held his hands out to pull me up.

"My first sorrow, I want it to be something huge," I said. " My biggest and my last."

My palm itched where ants had gotten on me. Even at that moment, I wanted to joke with him. I was drunk and I wanted to blow a raspberry on his arm to make him laugh.

"I have something to show you," he said as he pulled me up, the sky rushing down to meet me.

*

The barn door creaked with an ancient weight as we opened it. Inside was an old sailboat, the mast taken down so the boat would fit into the barn. The whole room whirled around, and I heard people outside saying goodbye to head home. Jackson pulled the cord to one bare bulb, while I drunkenly flopped up onto the chair of an old tractor.

He said, "It's my brother's old boat. He hasn't looked at it in years and he said if I could fix it, we could keep it."

"It's beautiful," I said. Already I could hear the ropes creaking in the lake wind, feel us sailing far past the shore, ignoring the siren song calling Jackson back. We could sail on the Great Lakes, large enough for shipwrecks and millennia of sorrow. In this dream, he's not swimming for shore.

I put my hand on his shirt and pushed it up to put my palm on the skin of his back. I pulled him to the tractor. I said, "Sit down."

"Oh, *really*," he said.

"Please sit down," I begged.

I pulled his shirt over his head as he sat in the tractor's seat. I straddled his lap, kissed him, and buried my face in his neck. The room was spinning. He kept his body taut, holding me so I wouldn't fall back, and his eyes were distant. I wanted to snap him out of it. I wanted to be the stone his fingers travelled over like a prayer bead. My hand itched where the ants had gotten it. I wanted to rub my palm on his skin. I wanted to give him any gift he named.

"Pretend I'm June," I said.

He pulled my hands down from around his neck. "Stop," he said. He put his hand to the scar in his hairline, his fingertips brushing past it.

"It's just a game. Call me June."

"Why is everything a game with you? This is not a game. This is real."

His hard-on grew underneath me. He said, "I don't even think of her anymore."

"June," I said. "June. I already know."

He clung to me so hard he was smothering me. "Please stop," he said.

Already I could see I wouldn't stop pushing until he said it out loud, until he drove himself to that stranger's feet, calling out her name at her window. I wouldn't stop following him down the sidewalk while he went looking for her, while he pleaded with her. Why couldn't it have been me?

My hand felt gritty, like I'd fallen on the pavement and sand had gotten embedded in my palm, and suddenly I knew what was happening. The grit was growing into a pebble right before my eyes—the kind of sorrow that comes on quick.

Jackson lifted me off him. Outside, drunken voices were whooping and hollering. He tried to hold my hand, to cover the stone so that neither of us could see it. But it pushed against him and our fingers were pulled apart. We heard our names being called. Crickets started their pulsing countdown.

Then Panda and the rest of Jackson's friends swept into the barn. I was still staring at my hand. They could all see it, what had grown there.

Samantha cupped my hand, rested her cheek to the cool stone. I could tell she had taken pills, the world numb and wondrous. They all trembled around me.

Lake, lake, lake, they started chanting.

I could barely stand to resist, and they set me on top of the sailboat. Jackson helped, taking hold under my armpit. He didn't want to let go, but whatever I was, I was not a stone, not an anchor. I was not enough. He did not climb up with me.

"I have to take a walk," he said.

Panda grabbed the chain hooked to the hitch the sailboat rested on and started pulling. "Oh," he said, "my back!" But he kept pulling. The rest of them joined up with much cheering, a procession pulling that hitch, rolling the sailboat down the shadowed road to the lake. I lay down on the deck, the sun already set, the green light of dusk spinning above me.

At the lakeshore, they lifted me down to place my feet on others' sorrows, the stones worn so smooth they felt like glass. The lake lapped at us in the gaps, the world veined with water. I could see Jackson's sister farther down the shore, holding her two little boys' hands, performing the daily ritual of waiting.

They lifted me off, and Barbie and others kneeled at my feet, hands cupped underneath me to catch the stone if it fell. I knew the lore: if you could catch a sorrow mid-air, just as it was breaking loose and before it touched the shore, you might be able to escape the lake's pull. Jackson did not join them. He started walking down the shore, and my heart reached for him. He bent to pick up a stone.

"He's found his," I said.

Panda said, "That's June's stone."

The rock was forming out of pieces of me, and the pieces were being dragged out. I held out my palm, my offering to everything we'd lost. All those people, those sorrows, shoring up that great lake. The waves kept beating, not the biggest wave, not the last, all that water polishing those stones to glass.

I could already see my sorrow clearly, how I would be tied to this place even when Jackson had left. His parents would let me sleep on their couch after he had gone. I would learn a heavy laugh, like gravel. When Jackson came back into town, called back by his stone, he wouldn't come to see me. I'd have to show up at the one bar in town when Samantha silently dragged me there, and Jackson would turn away from me with that tight-lipped smile I had learned to love. Of course I would laugh. I would close my eyes and laugh.

Human Value

by Emile DeWeaver

A friend recently told me, "We in the Humanities can
expect to make no money." She spoke with self-
deprecating humor, as does everyone I know in the humanities when they talk about their work. They grew up in the
same culture as I did, where schools balanced budgets by
cutting art first (and I include art here because art is a part
of the humanities, though it often stands alone). Perhaps
my humanities friends had a dad like mine whose response
to artistic aspirations was, "Heck no, Emile. It's hard
enough to be black; you're not going to be a black painter."
Whatever their backgrounds, they're accustomed to a
popular culture that devalues their work, because, unlike
the sciences, whose products are readily quantified in pa-
tients and dollars, the humanities resist commodification a
lot better than they do budget cuts.

How might we quantify the value of philosophy, history, or literature: what are they worth? I'd like to argue that
the humanities should defy quantification in a similar way
that human life should defy quantification, but I'll ballpark
a dollar amount: $16 billion dollars. Just kidding. $16 bil-

lion dollars is just how much an emphasis on humanities might save us in reduced prison expenditures.

I'm going to tell you a story, which isn't exactly scientific evidence, about the humanities' role in my transformation and rehabilitation. If we had time, I'd tell you about the hundreds of incarcerated men I know who also found a means of transformation through arts and humanities. I ask that you allow my story to represent them all—insomuch as the humanities can prove a powerful tool in both the rehabilitation of those who've broken society's norms and the habilitation of those who have never learned the norms.

By the time I was 18 years old, I was on track to a life sentence in prison for murder. My life and the lives of my victim's family were in ruin because the worldview I'd adopted was ruinous. Today, my worldview is life-affirming. That transformation didn't happen because 20 years ago prison "cured" me. My daughter played a big part in my change, but literature also played a pivotal role in reconnecting me with my humanity.

The book that changed my life was *Journals of Ralph Waldo Emerson*. In one journal, Emerson advocates, "Write your own Bible." His disillusionment with institutionalized religion spoke to me. Having long ago rejected church as an ethical authority, on trial for crimes committed for the ideals my friends in "the streets" held holy, I was disillusioned with everything. I had lost my ethic. This wasn't the first or even the second time I'd suffered this kind of disillusionment, and this exacerbated the instability in my already chaotic life.

An insecure childhood disposed me to seek security, and fundamental to my sense of security was a worldview.

The existential crisis I faced during my trial was that not only had I lost faith in the street ethic, but disillusionment left me too afraid to adopt any ethic at all. I'd followed other people's views all my life. They'd led me down different tracks to the same cell. Although I wasn't the kind of person who could thrive without an ethic, I was finished fitting myself into other people's perspectives. Until I read Emerson, it hadn't occurred to me to investigate what was important to me and create my own ethic from the thoughts of man. Philosophy, history, and world religion would consume me.

If I was going to forge my own ethic, I needed to understand what had come before me, what people had gotten right, and which answers had become antiquated. I sought the power of knowledge, but I found more than that. I'd wasted my life inhabiting different personas because I'd believed something was wrong with me, but in literature, I found something as transformative as it was surprising: validation of who I am, a secular humanist. In great minds from Emerson to Iyanla Vanzant, Lao Tzu to Khalil Gibran, I glimpsed reflections of myself. In literature, I rediscovered questions and ideas I'd had as a child, arguments that would have had me beaten for insolence or blasphemy. I felt at home among history's mental giants, and reading them made me feel gigantic. More than that, I felt like less of a social outcast, like I authoritatively belonged to the human race. This conviction made the difference between sinking beneath new lows of criminality and climbing toward a sense of world citizenship.

Even at 19 years old, I recognized the power of what I was reading. I remember closing Anthony T. Browder's

Nile Valley Contributions to Civilization—which for me re-wrote the narrative of what it meant to be black—and complaining to my cellmate, "Why the fuck weren't they teaching this in school?" I was angry because I believed that had I read Emerson and Gibran and Plato in junior high school, I would've thought and behaved differently. But there are no do-overs. I knew that all too well, so I resolved to move forward and write my Bible.

Talk to the kids who triumph over their environments, the superheroes, and although multiple factors will have contributed to their success, you'll likely discover in them the ingredients of a Herculean ethic: they have a strong vision of who they are, who they want to be, and what they believe. They've written their Bibles.

After I chased red herrings through Socrates' discursive investigations in *Dialogues of Plato,* I opened my blank book—permit me some artistic license here—and penned the first verse. *In the Beginning, Emile decided, "I shall be skeptical."*

I ingested thousands of pages of Chinese philosophy and learned about equanimity and compassion, meditation and karma. The latter especially appealed to me. Karma meant I lived in a world where I controlled my destiny, and this philosophy didn't ask me to believe in it. It asked me to examine cause and effect in my life and challenged me to deny or confirm the operation of karma. *Verse 2: And on the evening of the second day, Emile decided, "I shall not be a victim of circumstance."* Certainly bad things happen to good people, certainly social injustice is real, but you get from life what you put into it: hate reaps hate, love reaps love. We create the real world in which we live. Conversely, we can decline to create our worlds, in which case we will live in the world others have created for us.

I read Hindu literature. *Verse 3: We're all on the same journey; we're just at different bends in the road. Contempt for someone's character flaws makes no more sense than contempt for a stranger because she's traveling three days behind me. Contempt for myself makes less sense.*

Verse 4: I shall not sell what I can give away.

Verse 5: I do not choose who loves me. But if I'm honest about who I am, someone will.

Verse 6: If I write what I'm afraid to say, I can liberate those who also feel afraid to use their own voices to say the same things.

I wrote a whole Book of my Bible called "Folly of Kings," inspired by Marcel Duchamp's infamous sculpture, a toilet bowl that he placed on display and named *The Fountain*. I was 23 years old, and the sculpture made me angry because, in my mind, it didn't even look like a fountain. I didn't get it—I was thinking about decorative fountains with water-spitting features—so I castigated Duchamp in a paper I was writing for a college correspondence course. Halfway through my academic rant, I returned to my picture of *The Fountain* to stoke my self-righteousness, and an image flashed through my head. I was drinking water in a middle school in Los Angeles, and the drinking fountain looked just like Duchamp's sculpture. I realized the failure hadn't been in Duchamp's art but in my own mind. *Verse 7: And the spirit of Duchamp said, "Never hold someone accountable for your shortcomings. And never forget—you have shortcomings!"*

I named my favorite Book after my favorite writer: "Gibran." *Verse 8: Have the courage to be afraid.*

I read Mark Twain's "The Man that Corrupted Hadleyburg," a short story about the value of untested virtue, and realized that whatever ethic I forged would be as superficial as the morals of Hadleyburg's citizens if I didn't practice my ethic in the world. Up until this time, I'd become a hermit, spending most of my time away from prison politics, studying in solitude. It was like a strange twist on Plato's cave allegory. I'd spend years creating a different world for myself in my cell. This world was valuable—it's the foundation of my convictions today—but separated from life among people, it could only be a pseudo world of shadows. So I ascended from my cave into the light—for the light will always be found among people and not upon the esoteric heights of intellect.

In thousands of neighborhoods like Brownsville in Brooklyn, like [insert the hundred neighborhoods you know], social pressures condemn as many as 80 percent of the children to grow up and go to prison. These pressures include situated identity (a psychological phenomena by which a person becomes a criminal when treated like a criminal) and group conformity (peer pressure). Philip Zimbardo, creator of the Stanford Prison Experiment, characterizes the effort necessary to overcome pressure like these as heroic. The 20 percent success rate—we'll call it the rate of escape—of people in aforementioned neighborhoods support Zimbardo's assessment, and though I don't think it's fair kids need to be superheroes to break cycles of violence and incarceration, that's the state of our nation.

Granted this necessity, the meaningful question is, how do we make superheroes out of our kids?

If you listen to kids who are dropping out of school and joining the pipeline to prison, you'll often find that they lack a cogent vision of who they are, who they want to be, and what they believe. Talk to those who triumph over their environments, the superheroes, and although multiple factors will have contributed to their success, you'll likely discover in them the ingredients of a Herculean ethic: they have a strong vision of who they are, who they want to be, and what they believe. They've written their Bibles.

I had none of these ingredients through most of my teens, but when I closed my books to test my ethic in a maximum security prison—read: war zone 24 hours a day—I emerged from my cave with a clarity of identity that protected me from many of prison's pressures. Despite my need for acceptance, I didn't join a gang. Despite my fear in a dangerous place, I refused to own or carry a knife. Despite the prison politics that demanded—on pain of death—participation in racial riots, I never committed violence in a riot. I resisted prison's pressures because I knew who I was. I was clear about my values, and the humanities played a foundational role in this clarity.

Verse 9: In his 35th year, Emile cried for help. He finally understood, "I cannot make it alone. And if I could, what would be the point of getting there?"

Verse 10: Emile spoke; people listened. Emile realized, "I can change the world by talking about the change in me."

I might have had a different life if I'd read *Journals of Ralph Waldo Emerson* when I was 15 and still in school rather than when I was 19 on my way to prison. I think about those impoverished communities where only two in ten will have the Superhuman ethic to resist what most human beings won't, and I wonder if a stronger emphasis on arts and humanities in junior high school would give two more kids the clarity to transcend their social environments.

Two more kids in ten would raise the rate of escape from 20 to 40 percent. If this can translate into 20 percent fewer people in American prisons, that's 460,000 lives—460,000 families—rescued. If this translates into spending 20 percent less than the $80 billion dollars we spend annually on prisons, then we come back around to my ballpark figure. What might the humanities be worth outside Plato's cave, inside America's at-risk neighborhoods? $16 billion dollars?

The Inner Lives of Salad Forks
by Adriana Gardella

"Somebody's going to have to share," I said to the eight utensils assembled in the dishwasher's silverware basket, one per compartment. I towered over them, dangling a recently used cereal spoon. A butter knife occupied an end stall near the dishwasher door. "You're getting a roommate, buddy," I said, dropping the new arrival into place. The knife recoiled. The spoon felt like a pariah. For as long as I can remember, my world has been alive with inanimate objects.

In third grade, my desk sheltered weary pencil people who rested their heads on puffy, pink eraser pillows. Trashy Veronica, the flamboyantly violet ten-speed I rode as a teenager, lived in the garage and was a constant embarrassment. I wondered if my tendency to anthropomorphize made me a freak, or part of a weird community.

"I do that too," said my sister in Los Angeles after I described my one-sided dialogue with my dishwasher's inhabitants. "Except I think the utensils hate being alone. I feel bad when one is by itself and the rest have company," she said. At the time, she shared her home with a husband, a toddler and several houseplants. I'd lived by myself for twelve years.

"But it's like having a roommate," I protested. "They must hate sharing such close quarters."

"You just feel like that because you live in New York. I think spending time in the dishwasher is more like going to lunch with a friend."

While geography may have influenced our conflicting interpretations, I wanted to unearth the root of our perspective. Sitting in my mother's suburban kitchen, I sought answers as she attacked the contents of the sink, her rubber-gloved hands sanitizing each plate before its journey to the dishwasher. The silverware basket looked forbiddingly full.

"No," she said, as she jammed a pair of salad tongs into an occupied compartment. "I don't think about silverware that way." She turned with a smile. "For me, it's the glasses." She flung open a kitchen cabinet to reveal shelves of neatly ordered goblets, tumblers and mugs. "Whenever I use one, I know the others are jealous. It's not fair. The back row never gets a chance." She concluded, "The apple doesn't fall far from the tree."

From behind his newspaper, my stepfather said, "You people are nuts." He echoed the view expressed in an old Ikea commercial that departed from the kitchen and began with a woman abandoning a goose-necked desk lamp near a garbage heap on a rainy night. The wind howled. Sad music played. Then came a disembodied male voice. "If any of you feel sorry for this lamp that is because you are crazy. It has no feelings and the new one is much better," he said.

I suspected neither genetics nor insanity explained these feelings, and decided to investigate. Following an online request for sources, my inbox soon overflowed with evidence that, beyond my immediate family, the practice of attributing human emotions to things thrived.

One woman expelled déclassé volumes from her bookshelf because, "to stand next to them would upset the literature," she explained.

Another brought me back to the kitchen. "The fork is a boy, the knife is a man and the spoon is a girl," she said. "Every time I set a table, I imagine the girl wants to be near the plate, not on the outside as if she's defending the knife." Most of that made sense to me. Still I wondered, *Why doesn't she see that the spoon, with her sleek pageboy, is a grown woman?*

Psychologist Adam Waytz, an associate professor of management and organizations at Northwestern University's Kellogg School of Management, couldn't answer that question. But having spent nearly ten years studying the topic of anthropomorphism, he offers explanations for the phenomenon and believes there are critical reasons to seek to understand it.

Waytz suspects everyone anthropomorphizes inanimate objects and forces to some degree. The metaphoric language commonly used to describe stock markets as climbing and economies as ailing, support his view. Waytz says anthropomorphizing "is the simplest way to understand phenomena we're not familiar with." We treat them like what we know best—ourselves. After all, we don't know what it's like to be a dog—or a piece of cutlery.

Waytz and his colleagues have written numerous articles that detail how we benefit from attributing human characteristics to animals or inanimate objects or phenomena. They say it can help us feel more connected socially, especially if we're feeling isolated. Consider, for example, the relationship Tom Hanks's character established with a bloody volleyball in the movie *Castaway*.

Yet this explanation strikes me as inadequate to explain my lifelong responses to the objects with which I interact, regardless of my mood or social status. I find more compelling another, which Waytz and his co-authors articulate in "On Seeing Human: A Three-Factor Theory of Anthropomorphism." They write that effectance motivation, the desire to master one's environment, can also drive us to anthropomorphize. It's a way to create structure and reduce the anxiety that comes with uncertainty. Knowing I've done my best to give all my utensils their own chamber does, in fact, give me peace.

That's nice. But why has Waytz devoted much of the past decade to this seemingly quirky topic? He says it has important implications for several fields beyond psychology, including technology, the law and health care. For example, his studies show that technology appears better able to perform as intended when it seems to possess a human-like mind. At a time when people must interact with a dizzying range of technology, at home, at work, in their cars and beyond, this suggests there are meaningful consequences to humanizing it.

Anthropomorphism is also relevant to legal systems, which may determine guilt or innocence based on beliefs regarding the ability of an agent to act intentionally. Likewise, rights determinations often hinge on the perceived capacities of the agent—whether animal, fetus or psychopath. Anthropomorphism's implications for the law touch, most obviously, on issues including animal rights, euthanasia, abortion and capital punishment.

Waytz says even the weakest forms of anthropomorphism matter because the tendency to ascribe human characteristics to non-human entities has been shown to influence behavior. "Even if people 'know' the entity in question is not human, they still treat it as such," he says. For example, in "The War on Prevention," professors from the University of Michigan and the University of Southern California explore how warlike cancer metaphors can hinder prevention. Their research suggests that, when people believe they are fighting an enemy, they are less apt to limit their own risk-increasing behaviors, like smoking.

Finally, the more we understand the process by which we humanize objects, the more we will learn about the inverse process of dehumanization. Or as psychotherapist Tina Tessina told me, "People who treat objects as people are happier and more successful than people who treat people as objects, because their relationship with the inanimate makes the world seem friendlier and more welcoming."

Still, sometimes the relationship ends violently. "Everyday objects constantly conspire against us," said one man, who was eager to share his experience. He remembered shaking with rage after a willful wineglass shattered on his poured concrete floor. "Look at you now, smartglass! You're in a hundred pieces and you're going to be recycled."

Heaven

by Mike O'Mary

It was a spur-of-the-moment thing:

"Put on your winter coat and get a warm blanket," I told my daughter. "We're going out to look at Christmas lights."

When I was a kid, one of the highlights of the holiday season was driving around town looking at everyone's Christmas decorations. Our family—seven kids and two adults—would pile into the station wagon and off we'd go.

Normally, my father and a car full of kids was a volatile mixture. But it was different at Christmas. When you put us in our pajamas, wrapped us in our blankets, and took us out for a late-night ride to look at Christmas decorations, it was actually peaceful in that station wagon.

But that was then. My days of riding around in pajamas and blankets are pretty much over. However, one of the privileges of being a parent is that your children provide you with a legitimate excuse to do some of the things you haven't done since you were a kid. And so, we set out in search of wonderful, awe-inspiring Christmas lights.

Unfortunately, things seldom go according to plan when you try to recreate your childhood. Some little variable always changes the equation, sometimes for the better, sometimes for worse. Such was the case that evening when I took Kathleen, my little six-year-old variable, out for a Christmas drive.

I had in mind a little subdivision in the neighboring town of Sycamore, Illinois, about five miles from our house. My wife and I had gone there earlier that week for a Christmas party, and we both thought it was nice that everybody in the neighborhood had decorated their homes. However, rather than drive through Sycamore to the subdivision as I had done with my wife, I decided to save time by taking the back roads. It turned out to be a bad choice.

We saw a few decorations at farmsteads en route, and when we got a little north of Sycamore, I turned down a road that I thought would lead to the subdivision. I was wrong. We drove around for half an hour without seeing any lights at all, let alone Christmas lights. However, while we were lost, we had a very interesting conversation:

"Daddy," Kathleen asked, "Do you believe in Santa?"

"Do you?" I asked.

"Yes," she said.

"Then I do, too," I said.

My answer seemed to be acceptable. Score one for Daddy. Soon came another question.

"Do you believe in God?" she asked.

This one caught me off guard. I'm sorry to say despite attending St. Elizabeth Elementary School and serving as an altar boy, and despite a higher education that included exposure to Hinduism, Buddhism, existential philosophy and the theological writings of Paul Tillich, I was not prepared to give my daughter a definitive answer at that moment. I had never been able to assimilate any of the things I learned into a set of beliefs that made much sense to me, and it seemed to me that an appropriate answer would require a lengthy discussion of abstract and complex theological and philosophical thought. And after all that, it still pretty much comes down to a leap of faith.

The thought of trying to explain all of this to my daughter in a few simple words seemed overwhelming. However, in all my feeble reflections on the subject of religion and God, Being and Non-Being, I have come to one conclusion: I do not believe that there is nothing—which implies that I must believe that there is something. And so, I took a leap that night and provided my daughter with a slightly boiled-down version of what would otherwise have been a very lengthy and probably confusing answer.

"Yes," I said.

Her response: "I do, too."

There was a short pause, then: "Daddy, do you believe in heaven?"

I thought for a moment. "I believe we will always be together," I said.

"I think Pop is in heaven," said Kathleen.

Pop was Kathleen's great grandfather. He had died earlier that year after a long illness.

"It made Grandma sad when Pop died," she continued.

"Yes, it did," I said.

"I know what Grandma's mom's name was," she said. "It was Gram."

"That's right," I said.

"I liked Pop," said Kathleen. Then she added, "It's not nice to make fun of old people."

"No, it's not."

There was another short pause.

"Everybody dies, even if they don't think they will," said Kathleen.

There was no skirting this comment. "Yes, that's true," I said.

In all my feeble reflections on the subject of religion and God, Being and Non-Being, I have come to one conclusion: I do not believe that there is nothing—which implies that I must believe that there is something.

We drove along the blacktop highway, cutting across the countryside. I hadn't noticed it until then, but at some point it had started to snow—big, heavy, wet flakes. Other than that, it was a very still, dark December night. My daughter was quiet for a long time, but she was alert, looking out the window, thinking hard. Finally, she spoke again.

"I'm a little bit afraid of dying," said Kathleen.

Fear of dying ... at last, a subject that I knew something about.

"A lot of people are afraid of dying," I said, "because we don't know what's it's going to be like."

"Yeah, we don't know what it's going to be like in the ground or if we'll go to heaven," she said.

I did not want her to have nightmares about being in the ground. "You don't actually go in the ground," I told her. "Your body does, but by then you've left your body."

She thought about this, and then said, "I don't get you."

"That's okay," I said. "Wherever you go, I'll be there." This I truly believed. I could not imagine any circumstances, even death, that would cause me to drift very far from my daughter.

"And Pop will be there," said Kathleen. "And Gram."

"That's right."

The conversation went on like that for a while longer. I was a little angry with myself for not being more prepared for such a conversation, but I was pleased to see that her mind was already at work on some of life's biggest questions. I took comfort in the realization that my daughter would probably be able to figure out most things for herself—which means she'll be a lot better off in the long run than she would be if she relied on someone like her father to figure things out for her.

While all this was going on, I was still not finding the neighborhood. At some point I realized that Kathleen didn't really know why we were driving around. When I said we were going "to look at Christmas lights," she thought I meant that we were going to a store to buy more lights for the Christmas tree. By the time she figured out the real purpose of our trip, she was pretty tired. When I finally found the neighborhood, she was asleep.

It was just as well. On second glance, the decorations in the neighborhood seemed ordinary and unimaginative. There was nothing particularly wonderful or awe-inspiring about them. I drove around for a little while, but by then I was tired, too, so I turned around and headed home.

The whole excursion could have been pretty depressing. I had wanted to show my daughter some wonderful Christmas lights. Instead, I got lost. Then, when I finally found the neighborhood, the lights were nothing special. It was a far cry from the memories I had of driving around, looking at decorations when I was a kid. But that's okay. We had discussed Santa and God and heaven and death—a conversation I would not soon forget. And at the end of the evening, I was heading home while my daughter slept like an angel in the seat next to me. I would not trade that drive with my daughter for anything.

Just then, Kathleen opened her eyes a little.

"Daddy?" she asked.

"Yes?" I answered.

She didn't answer right away. I looked over at her. She looked very warm and cozy—very peaceful—the way a child in warm pajamas and a blanket should look when out for a Christmas drive with her father.

"Yes," I repeated softly. "What is it?"

"Maybe this is heaven," she said.

I thought about that for a moment.

"Yes," I said. "Maybe it is."

"Heaven" originally appeared in *The Chicago Tribune Sunday Magazine.*

Contributors

Lauren Camp is the author of three poetry books about dislocation, jazz, landscape, visual art, longing, treachery, politics and home. They include *This Business of Wisdom*, *The Dailiness*, and most recently *One Hundred Hungers*, for which she received a Dorset Prize. Camp's poetry has appeared in *World Literature Today*, *At Length*, *Beloit Poetry Journal*, and as a Poem-a-Day for Poets.org.

Jeremy Cantor began writing poetry shortly before retiring from a career in laboratory chemistry. His debut collection, *Wisteria From Seed*, was published in 2015 by Kelsey Books.

Marie Chambers received an MFA from Bennington College. Her work has appeared in *The LA Review of Books*, *The Atlanta Review*, *Talking Writing*, *The Quotable*, *The Ilanot Review*, and elsewhere. She won the 2014 Tallahassee Writers Association annual prize for creative non-fiction and the 2015 ARTlines2 Ekphrastic Poetry Contest for work inspired by a piece of art at the Museum of Fine Arts in Houston. Most recently her collaboration with Paris-based visual artist Daniela Bershon was featured in the online magazine *7 x 7*.

Alexandra Comeaux earned an MFA in Creative Writing at Arizona State University. She works as a filmmaker and writer in Phoenix, Arizona. Her work has been recently published in *Quarter After Eight* and *Southwest Review*.

Valerie Cumming received her MFA in Creative Writing from the University of Michigan in 2002; since then, her stories have appeared or are forthcoming in nearly thirty publications. She is currently a freelance writer, teacher, and editor based in Columbus, Ohio, where she lives with her husband and four daughters.

Joseph Dante is a writer and editor from South Florida. His work has previously appeared in *Permafrost*, *The Rumpus*, *PANK*, *Pear Noir!*, *Corium*, and elsewhere.

Emile DeWeaver is a Contributing Editor for *Easy Street*. His work has appeared or is forthcoming at *The Lascaux Review*, *Your Impossible Voice*, *The Seventh Wave*, *Drunk Monkeys*, and *The Rumpus*. He lives and writes in Northern California.

Joe Dornich is a PhD candidate in Texas Tech's creative writing program, where he also serves as Managing Editor for *Iron Horse Literary Review*. Joe's stories have won contests with the South Central Modern Language Association, *The Masters Review*, Fresher Publishing, and *Carve Magazine*.

Lydia Fitzpatrick's work has appeared in the The *O. Henry Prize Stories 2016*, *The Best American Mystery Stories 2016*, *One Story*, *Glimmer Train*, and *Mid-American Review*. She's been awarded the Carl Djerassi Fiction Fellowship at the Wisconsin Institute for Creative Writing, an Elizabeth George Foundation Grant, and a Wallace Stegner Fellowship in Fiction at Stanford University. She has taught creative writing at the University of Michigan, the University of Wisconsin-Madison, and through Stanford's Continuing Studies Program. She lives in Los Angeles with her husband and two daughters and is working on her first novel.

April Ford served as a guest editor for the Pushcart Prize Anthology XLI. Her short story "Project Fumarase" is among the winning pieces in the previous anthology XL. April's debut story collection, *The Poor Children* (SFWP), was published in 2015, and her debut novel, *Carousel*, is forthcoming in 2019 (Inanna Publications). She splits her time between Canada and the US. Her website is aprilfordauthor.com

Adriana Gardella is a lawyer-turned-writer who created, and for several years wrote, an online *New York Times* column. She also contributed numerous articles and an essay to the paper's print edition. Her work has appeared in a wide range of publications, living and dead, including *National Geographic Traveler*, *Newsweek*, *The New York Observer* and *Salon*. An excerpt from her memoir about work will appear in the Winter 2018 issue of *Broad Street*. She lives in New York.

Mary Hennessy's work has appeared in *The Independent*, *The News & Observer*, and *Windhover*, the literary journal of North Carolina State University, and has been read on the R-Busline in Raleigh, North Carolina and in the play "Deployed."

Kathryn Bucolo Hill's flash fiction and short stories have appeared in *AGNI Online*, *Juked*, *Passages North*, and elsewhere. She received an MFA in fiction from Arizona State University.

Jackleen Holton Hookway's poems and stories have been published in the anthologies *The Giant Book of Poetry*, and *Steve Kowit: This Unspeakably Marvelous Life*, and have appeared or are forthcoming in *Atlanta Review*, *Natural Bridge*, *North American Review*, *Rattle*, *Sanskrit*, and elsewhere. In 2014, her poem "Goldfish" won Bellingham Review's 49th Parallel Poetry Award.

Born in Brown County, Texas, Landon Houle currently lives and works in South Carolina. Her writing has won contests at *Black Warrior Review*, *Crab Creek Review*, and *Permafrost*, and her story "Travelers" was recently named a Pushcart Prize special mention. Other work has appeared or is forthcoming in *Baltimore Review*, *Crazyhorse*, *Natural Bridge*, *Harpur Palate*, *River Styx* and elsewhere.

Ronald Jackson writes stories, poems, and nonfiction. His work has appeared in *The Chattahoochee Review*, *Kentucky Review*, *Painted Bride Quarterly*, *Prime Number Magazine*, *Vine Leaves Literary Journal*, and elsewhere. He lives in Durham, NC.

Amanda Kabak is the author of the novel *The Mathematics of Change* and has had stories published in *Arcturus Review*, *Midwestern Gothic*, *Sequestrum*, and other print and online periodicals. She was the recipient of *Arcturus Review's* Al Simak's award for fiction as well as the Betty Gabehard prize, issued by the Kentucky Women Writer's Conference. She has been nominated for several Pushcart Prizes and holds an MFA from Pacific University.

Colette Langlois was raised in Canada's Northwest Territories and has lived most of her life there when not otherwise wandering the blue-green planet. "The Emigrants," imagined on the Isle of Iona, written in the Colorado Rockies, and edited in the Algarve, was her first fiction publication, and was awarded the 2016 Writers' Trust of Canada/McClelland & Stewart Journey Prize. She currently resides in the Yukon Territory, where she is working on a short story collection and a novel.

Ríona Judge McCormack was the 2016 Hennessy New Irish Writer of the Year, the recipient of the 2017 Sunday Business Post Short Story Prize, and was awarded the inaugural Galley Beggar Press Short Story Prize. Her work has been published in *The Irish Times*, *The Dublin Review*, the *Aesthetica Creative Writing Annual* and other international anthologies, and broadcast nationwide on Ireland's RTE Radio One.

Ed McManis's poems have appeared in numerous journals including *Piedmont Review*, *California Quarterly*, *Rhino*, and *Blue Road Reader*. His most recent chapbook is *Working For My Old Man*. He runs a small school in San Francisco for students who learn differently.

Martha Miller is the author of six published books: *Skin to Skin: Erotic Lesbian Love Stories*, *Nine Nights on the Windy Tree*, *Dispatch to Death*, *Tales from the Levee*, *Retirement Plan*, and *Widow*. Her stories, reviews, and articles are widely published in anthologies, periodicals, and newspapers. She writes a monthly column for Out and About Illinois called "Martha [Lesbian] Living," a lesbian send-up of that other, more domestic, Martha. She is a winner of a Raymond Carver Short Fiction Award and the Illinois Arts Council Artists Fellowship, among others.

Darren Morris's publications include *The American Poetry Review*, *The Missouri Review*, *The Southern Review*, *New England Review*, *Best New Poets*, and others.

Van Newell received his MFA from Columbia University and currently teaches at the University of Alabama. He is the winner of the Hackney award and an award from the Alabama Writers Conclave. His writing has been published in *Medium*, *New Guard Review*, *Weld*, *Postscript*, *Cumulus*, and elsewhere.

Timothy O'Leary's most recent collection is *Dick Cheney Shot Me in the Face, and Other Tales of Men in Pain*. He is the author of the non-fiction book *Warriors, Workers, Whiners, & Weasels*. His fiction and essays have been published in dozens of magazines, journals, and anthologies. He won the Aestas Short Story Award and was a finalist for the Mississippi Review Prize and the Mark Twain Award for humor writing. Born in Billings, MT, he graduated from the University of Montana and received his MFA from Pacific University. More information can be found at timothyolearylit.com.

Mike O'Mary is author of *Wise Men and Other Stories* and *The Note*. He is also the founder of Dream of Things, which publishes memoirs and anthologies, including *Saying Goodbye: to the people, places and things in our lives*. Mike has published stories and essays in the Sunday magazines of *The Chicago Tribune*, *Denver Post*, *Rocky Mountain News*, *Baltimore Sun*, *Cleveland Plain Dealer*, and *Detroit Free Press*. He is a graduate of the University of Montana (MFA in Creative Writing, MA in English Literature) and the Second City Comedy Writing Program.

Brenda Peynado's stories have been selected for the O. Henry Prize Stories 2015, and won prizes from the Nelson Algren Award, Glimmer Train Fiction Open Contest, and others. Her work appears or is forthcoming in *The Georgia Review*, *The Threepenny Review*, *Ecotone*, *EPOCH*, *Mid-American Review*, and elsewhere. She received her MFA from Florida State University and her Ph.D. from the University of Cincinnati, and she is currently teaching at the University of Central Florida.

David Salner worked for 25 years as an iron ore miner, steelworker, and general laborer. His writing has appeared in *Threepenny Review*, *Lascaux Review*, *Iowa Review*, *Prairie Schooner*, *Salmagundi*, and many other magazines. His third book is *Blue Morning Light* and features poems on the paintings of American artist George Bellows. He has an MFA degree from the University of Iowa.

JL Schneider is a carpenter and an adjunct professor of English at a small community college in upstate New York. Winner of the 2015 Prism Review Poetry Contest, his poetry has also appeared in *Crazy River*, *The Taos Review*, *The Rhode Island Review*, *Slippery Elm*, and *Rolling Stone*, among others. His poetry collection *It's Strange Here* was recently published by Vine Leaves Press. You can visit him on the web at www.schneiderjl.com.

Kate E. Schultz earned her MA from Ohio University, where she also served as Assistant Editor of *New Ohio Review*. Her work has appeared in *Bayou Magazine*, *Midwestern Gothic*,

Eclipse: A Literary Journal, and others. She is currently Associate Editor of *Sow's Ear Poetry Review* and a Disability Services Advocate at Columbus State Community College.

DeAnna Stephens holds an MFA from George Mason University. Her poetry has been nominated twice for a Pushcart Prize and has appeared most recently in *PoetryRepairs* and *Canadian Woman Studies*. She teaches writing and literature at Roane State Community College in Crossville, Tennessee.

Neha Sud is a nomad, spending her life between four continents. Her work in international development has taken her to some of the most remote corners of the world. Writing is an experiment to find home. She focuses on flash fiction and prose, but can be convinced to take a leap into poetry. "How to Say Goodbye" is her first publication.

Elizabeth Vignali is an optician, writer, and co-producer of the Bellingham Kitchen Sessions reading series, and is the author of *Object Permanence* (Finishing Line Press). Her poems have appeared in *Willow Springs*, *Cincinnati Review*, *The American Journal of Poetry*, *Tinderbox*, *The Literary Review*, and elsewhere.

Cady Vishniac's poems have appeared in *Sugar House Review*, *Tupelo Quarterly*, and *Verse Daily*.

Jeff Walt's work has appeared in *The Sun*, *Connecticut Review*, *Inkwell*, *The Good Men Project*, *Cream City Review*, and elsewhere. He is a recipient of the Red Hen Poetry Prize, The Keystone Chapbook Prize (for *Soot*), and other honors.

Alexander Weinstein is the Director of The Martha's Vineyard Institute of Creative Writing and the author of the collection *Children of the New World* (Picador 2016). His stories have appeared in *Cream City Review, Notre Dame Review, Pleiades, PRISM International, Quarter After Eight, Sou'wester, Zone 3,* and other journals.